LIVING IN THE SHADOW OF THE BET

A Healing Workbook for Families Touched by a Loved One's Gambling

James Martinez
MS, LCADC, LSATP, CAADC, CASAC-II, ICGC

Stress Free Recovery LLC · United States · 2026

Living in the Shadow of the Bet: A Clinical Workbook for Families Affected by Gambling Addiction

Publisher: Stress Free Recovery LLC
Series: Evidence-Based Clinical Frameworks
Author: James Martinez, MS, LCADC, LSATP, CAADC, CASAC-II, ICGC
Edition: First Edition 2026
Format: Workbook · 8.5 × 11 inches · US
Credentials: MS (Master of Science) · LCADC (Licensed Clinical Alcohol and Drug Counselor) · LSATP (Licensed Substance Abuse Treatment Practitioner) · CAADC (Certified Advanced Alcohol and Drug Counselor) · CASAC-II (Credentialed Alcoholism and Substance Abuse Counselor, Level II) · ICGC (International Certified Gambling Counselor)

Stress Free Recovery LLC | United States

Printed in the United States of America

Table of Contents

Note: Page numbers are approximate and reflect the workbook's printed layout.

Introduction

Welcome Letter from the Author

Dear Reader,

If you have picked up this workbook, you are already doing something incredibly courageous. You are acknowledging that something in your life — in your family, your home, your heart — has been broken by gambling. You may have spent years minimizing the problem, making excuses for it, lying awake at night calculating how you will cover the next debt, or wondering which version of the person you love will walk through the door tonight. You have probably asked yourself, more times than you can count: *How did we get here?*

I want to begin by saying something clearly and without qualification: **This is not your fault.** Gambling disorder is a recognized, clinically significant mental health condition — not a moral failure, not a character flaw, and not something that happened because you were not enough. It is a disorder of the brain's reward system that hijacks the lives of everyone in its orbit. You are one of those people. And your experience, your pain, and your story matter deeply.

I have spent years working with individuals and families in the grip of addiction — including gambling addiction — and I have witnessed firsthand how profoundly this disorder devastates families from the inside out. I have sat with spouses who discovered six-figure debts they knew nothing about. I have worked with parents who bailed their adult children out of crisis so many times they had nothing left financially or emotionally. I have listened to the children of gamblers describe growing up in households defined by unpredictability, secrecy, and fear. Their stories are different in their details, but identical in their core truth: *love alone is not enough to save someone from addiction, but it is enough to destroy the person doing the saving if that person does not get help.*

This workbook was written specifically for **you** — the spouse, the partner, the parent, the sibling who has been living in the shadow of the bet. Every page was crafted with your healing in mind. You will find clinical education to help you understand what gambling disorder really is. You will find worksheets that invite you to name your experience honestly — perhaps for the first time. You will find tools drawn from the most evidence-based frameworks in the field: Cognitive Behavioral Therapy (CBT), Motivational Interviewing (MI), Community Reinforcement and Family Training (CRAFT), Trauma-Informed Care (TIC), and Solution-Focused Therapy. These are not theories designed for textbooks. They are practical, tested approaches that work — and they have been adapted here with you in mind.

You do not have to have it all figured out to begin. You do not have to have decided whether to stay or leave. You do not have to be ready to confront your loved one, or ready to forgive them, or ready to do anything except *open this book and begin.* Begin here. Begin today. Begin exactly as you are.

There is something important I want you to hold as you work through these pages: **hope is a clinical tool.** Research consistently shows that when family members engage in structured support and education — even without the gambler's participation — outcomes improve significantly. Your healing does not have to wait for theirs. In fact, when you heal, the entire system around you begins to shift. That is not wishful thinking. That is the evidence.

I am honored to walk with you through this process. You deserve support. You deserve clarity. You deserve a life that is not defined by someone else's addiction.

Let's begin.

With deep respect and genuine care,

James Martinez, MS, LCADC, LSATP, CAADC, CASAC-II, ICGC

Author | Stress Free Recovery LLC

How to Use This Workbook

This workbook is organized into **twelve modules**, each addressing a distinct and essential dimension of the experience of families affected by gambling addiction. The modules are designed to be completed sequentially, as each section builds on the insights and skills developed in previous ones — but if a particular topic is urgent for you right now, it is entirely appropriate to move to that section first and return to earlier material later.

Module Structure

Each module follows a consistent structure:

- **Clinical Rationale:** A brief explanation of why this topic matters and how it connects to your recovery and well-being.
- **What You Will Gain from This Module:** A clear, bulleted preview of skills, insights, or tools you will take away.
- **Educational Content:** Evidence-based psychoeducation written in accessible, plain language.
- **Worksheets:** Structured, fill-in exercises with clear instructions, labeled fields, and space for your responses.
- **Reflection Exercises:** Guided journaling prompts that invite deeper personal exploration.
- **Module Summary and Transition Prompt:** A closing summary and a bridge into the next section.

For Self-Guided Users

If you are using this workbook on your own, you are encouraged to move at a pace that feels manageable. There is no prescribed timeline. Some modules may take a single session; others may require you to return over several days. Keep a dedicated journal alongside this workbook for additional reflection space. Be gentle with yourself — this material is emotionally demanding, and it is normal to feel activated, sad, or overwhelmed at points. If this occurs, use the grounding exercises in Module 5 or step away for self-care before continuing.

For Group and Therapy Settings

This workbook is fully compatible with individual therapy, couples therapy, family therapy, and group formats such as Gam-Anon support groups or psychoeducational family groups. Clinicians are encouraged to assign specific modules as between-session work and process completed worksheets during sessions.

The reflection exercises serve as excellent clinical discussion prompts. Module 12 includes a collaborative worksheet designed specifically for use in conjoint sessions with the gambler.

A Note on Pacing

You do not need to complete this workbook in order, and you do not need to rush. Healing is not linear. It is okay to re-read sections, revisit completed worksheets, or take breaks between modules. This workbook will be here when you are ready.

A Note on Cultural Responsiveness

Gambling and its consequences do not occur in a cultural vacuum. The experience of having a loved one with a gambling problem is shaped profoundly by culture — by what a family believes about loyalty and obligation, by what gambling means within a community, by whether seeking help is seen as brave or shameful, by whether talking about family problems to an outsider is acceptable or taboo.

Across many cultures, there is a deep value placed on keeping family struggles private. In some communities, gambling is a normalized social activity — a way of participating in tradition, establishing social status, or bonding across generations. In others, the stigma around addiction of any kind can be so severe that family members suffer in complete isolation rather than seek help that might expose the secret. Religious and spiritual frameworks may also shape how family members interpret the gambler's behavior and their own role in responding to it.

This workbook was written with cultural humility at its center. The exercises and examples offered here are meant to serve as starting points — not prescriptions. You are the expert on your own cultural context, your family's values, and what feels possible and safe for you.

For Clinicians — Cultural Adaptation

When using this workbook with clients from diverse cultural backgrounds, take time to explore how cultural values around family loyalty, gender roles, shame, and help-seeking may shape the client's engagement with specific exercises. Invite clients to adapt prompts to fit their cultural framework. For example, a client whose cultural background emphasizes collective family well-being over individual healing may benefit from reframing self-care as "strengthening myself so I can better support my family." Always ask before assuming.

Whatever your background, wherever you come from, whatever your family has believed about gambling: **you belong here.** Your pain is real, your experience is valid, and this workbook was written for you.

A Note to Clinicians

This workbook is grounded in four primary evidence-based frameworks that have demonstrated clinical effectiveness with both addiction populations and their affected family members. A brief orientation to each framework will help clinicians use this material most effectively.

Framework	Clinical Application in This Workbook
Cognitive Behavioral Therapy (CBT)	Used throughout to help clients identify and restructure automatic thoughts that perpetuate enabling, shame, and self-blame. Thought record worksheets appear in Modules 3, 4, and beyond.
Motivational Interviewing (MI)	Informs the non-judgmental, client-centered tone of the workbook. The decisional balance exercises in Module 10 and the future-orientation exercises in Module 12 are directly MI-derived.
Community Reinforcement and Family Training (CRAFT)	Provides the behavioral framework for enabling reduction (Module 3), communication skills (Module 8), and supporting recovery (Module 12). CRAFT has strong empirical support for engaging treatment-resistant individuals through family training.
Trauma-Informed Care (TIC)	Informs the overall tone of safety, trustworthiness, and empowerment. Module 5 is dedicated to trauma psychoeducation. Grounding exercises appear

Framework	Clinical Application in This Workbook
	throughout. Clinicians are encouraged to always assess for trauma history before assigning emotionally activating material.
Solution-Focused Therapy	Used in future-oriented reflection exercises and in Module 12's vision work. Encourages clients to identify strengths and exceptions to problem-dominated narratives.

Clinicians should assess clients for significant trauma symptoms, suicidality, domestic violence risk, and co-occurring disorders prior to beginning this workbook. Module 5 includes a trauma symptom checklist and explicit instructions to pursue professional assessment when symptoms are significant. Module 10 includes domestic violence safety planning protocols.

Module 1

Understanding Gambling Addiction — What Families Need to Know

Clinical Rationale: Before a family member can begin to heal from the impact of someone else's gambling, they must first understand what gambling disorder actually is. Families are frequently given inaccurate, incomplete, or shame-laden information about addiction that leads to confusion, self-blame, and ineffective responses. This module provides clear, accessible psychoeducation grounded in the most current clinical and neuroscientific understanding of gambling disorder — not to excuse the gambler's behavior, but to help you make sense of what you have been experiencing.

What You Will Gain from This Module

- A clear understanding of what gambling disorder is and how it is diagnosed
- Insight into the brain chemistry behind gambling addiction and why the gambler behaves as they do
- Knowledge of how gambling addiction affects the entire family system
- A personal timeline worksheet to organize your experience and name the impact
- Exploration of your pre-existing beliefs and myths about gambling

1.1 What Is Gambling Disorder?

Gambling disorder is classified in the *Diagnostic and Statistical Manual of Mental Disorders, Fifth Edition* (DSM-5) as a behavioral addiction — the only behavioral addiction with its own diagnostic category. This classification reflects decades of neuroscientific research demonstrating that gambling disorder activates the same brain circuits, produces the same neurochemical responses, and follows the same progression of loss of control as substance use disorders. Understanding this is essential for families, because it means that what you have witnessed is not weakness, not choice, and not indifference to you — it is a disorder of the brain's reward system.

The DSM-5 Diagnostic Criteria — In Plain Language

According to the DSM-5 (American Psychiatric Association, 2013), gambling disorder is diagnosed when a person experiences **persistent and recurrent problematic gambling behavior** causing significant impairment or distress, demonstrated by **four or more** of the following nine criteria within a 12-month period:

#	Clinical Criterion	What It Looks Like in Real Life
1	Needs to gamble with increasing amounts of money to achieve desired excitement (tolerance)	The $20 bet that used to thrill them no longer does; now they need to bet hundreds or thousands.
2	Restless or irritable when attempting to cut down or stop (withdrawal)	Mood swings, agitation, anxiety when they haven't gambled — similar to withdrawal in substance use.
3	Repeated unsuccessful efforts to control, cut back, or stop gambling	Promises to stop that are not kept; short periods of stopping followed by relapse.
4	Often preoccupied with gambling	Conversations always come back to gambling; mentally absent even when physically present.
5	Often gambles when feeling distressed (escape gambling)	Uses gambling to cope with stress, depression, loneliness, boredom, or conflict.
6	After losing money, often returns to "get even" (chasing losses)	The belief that the next bet will recoup what was lost — a hallmark cognitive distortion of gambling disorder.
7	Lies to conceal the extent of involvement with gambling	Hidden accounts, falsified statements, lying about whereabouts, minimizing losses.
8	Has jeopardized or lost a significant relationship, job, or opportunity because of gambling	Job loss, estrangement from family members, missed events, broken commitments.

#	Clinical Criterion	What It Looks Like in Real Life
9	Relies on others to provide money to relieve desperate financial situations caused by gambling (bailout)	Borrowing from family, friends, employers; taking out loans; expecting family to cover debts.

Severity specifiers: Mild (4–5 criteria), Moderate (6–7 criteria), Severe (8–9 criteria).

The Brain Chemistry Behind Gambling Addiction

To understand why a gambler cannot "just stop," it helps to understand what gambling does to the brain. Gambling triggers a powerful release of **dopamine** — the brain's primary reward neurotransmitter — in a pattern that is actually more intense than many substances. Unlike a reliable chemical that produces a predictable high, gambling operates on what psychologists call a *variable-ratio reinforcement schedule* — the same mechanism that makes slot machines so addictive. The unpredictability of the reward is precisely what makes it so powerful; the brain becomes conditioned to crave the anticipation as much as the win.

Over time, the brain's reward circuitry is altered. The prefrontal cortex — responsible for impulse control, planning, and decision-making — becomes progressively less effective at overriding the compulsive drive to gamble. This is why the gambler can know intellectually that gambling is destroying their life and still find themselves unable to stop. It is the same neurological phenomenon that underlies all addiction.

The Addiction Cycle

Gambling addiction typically follows a recognizable cycle:

1. **Trigger:** Emotional distress, financial pressure, boredom, or opportunity
2. **Urge and Preoccupation:** Craving and mental planning around gambling
3. **Acting Out:** Gambling episode, often with escalating bets
4. **Guilt and Shame:** Remorse, self-recrimination, promises to stop
5. **Tension Building:** Stress, anxiety, and renewed craving — leading back to Step 1

Family members often find themselves caught in a parallel cycle of hope (during Step 4) and devastation (when Step 5 leads back to gambling). Understanding this cycle is not about excusing it; it is about no longer being blindsided by it.

1.2 How Gambling Addiction Affects the Whole Family — The Family Disease Model

---

Gambling disorder does not live in one person. It lives in the family. Family systems theory recognizes that when one member of a family system becomes dominated by addiction, every other member adapts — often in ways that are harmful to their own well-being — in order to maintain some semblance of stability. The term "family disease" does not mean that family members are sick; it means that the disorder creates ripple effects that touch every relationship, every role, and every corner of the home.

Roles Family Members Often Adopt

Role	Description	Internal Experience
The Caretaker / Hero	Takes on responsibility for managing the family's chaos; covers for the gambler; maintains outward appearance of normalcy.	Exhausted, resentful, hypervigilant; derives identity from being needed.
The Enabler	Provides money, makes excuses, shields the gambler from consequences — often motivated by love and fear.	Conflicted; believes they are helping while knowing something is wrong.
The Scapegoat	Often a child or other family member who acts out and draws attention away from the gambling problem.	Angry, misunderstood; their behavior is often a symptom of family distress.
The Lost Child	Withdraws, becomes invisible, asks for nothing so as not to add to the family's burden.	Lonely, disconnected, may carry unacknowledged grief and depression.
The Mascot	Uses humor to diffuse tension and relieve family stress; the "class clown" of the family system.	Anxious underneath; uses humor to manage their own fear and others' distress.

Reflection Prompt

As you read through the roles above, did any of them feel familiar — either as roles you have played, or roles you have seen others in your family play? You may have played more than one over time. There are no wrong answers here.

The Systemic Impact of Gambling Disorder on Families

Research consistently documents the following impacts on family members of problem gamblers:

- **Financial:** Depleted savings, hidden debts, bankruptcy, mortgage defaults, stolen funds
- **Emotional:** Depression, anxiety, anger, grief, shame, emotional exhaustion
- **Physical:** Stress-related illness, sleep disturbance, headaches, cardiovascular impact
- **Relational:** Erosion of trust, social isolation, sexual intimacy breakdown, parenting impairment
- **Intergenerational:** Children at elevated risk for their own gambling problems, anxiety disorders, and relationship difficulties in adulthood

---

1.3 Worksheet: What I Have Witnessed — My Family Gambling Timeline

WORKSHEET 1.3 — My Family Gambling Timeline

Instructions: Use the timeline below to record gambling-related events you have witnessed or experienced in chronological order. Include the approximate date, a brief description of the event, and how it affected you personally. You do not need to fill in every row. Start wherever your memory leads you. This exercise is for *your* clarity — not for confrontation or legal purposes.

Take your time. It may be helpful to close your eyes briefly before you begin and allow your memory to surface the key moments.

Date / Time Period	What I Witnessed or Experienced	How It Affected Me
First signs I noticed: ______ / ______		
Early escalation: ______ / ______		
First major financial crisis: ______ / ______		
First discovered lie: ______ / ______		
Major relationship rupture: ______ / ______		
Attempt(s) to stop: ______ / ______		
Relapse / return to gambling: ______ / ______		
Most recent crisis: ______ / ______		
Today: ______ / ______		

After completing your timeline, respond to the following:

What patterns do you notice looking at your timeline as a whole?

How long have you been living with this reality?

What has surprised you most about seeing this written out?

1.4 Reflection Exercise: What Did I Think Gambling Was?

Reflection Exercise 1.4 — Exploring My Beliefs About Gambling

Our cultural backgrounds, family histories, and personal experiences shape the beliefs we hold about gambling — what it is, who does it, and what it means. These beliefs powerfully influence how we respond to a loved one's gambling problem. This exercise invites you to examine those beliefs honestly.

Part 1: Common Myths About Gambling — Check Any You Have Believed

☐ "Gambling is just a bad habit, not a real addiction."

☐ "If they really loved me, they would stop."

☐ "Everyone gambles sometimes — it's not a big deal."

☐ "They're only hurting themselves."

☐ "A real win would fix everything."

☐ "I should have seen the warning signs sooner."

☐ "If I support them enough, they'll stop on their own."

☐ "Gambling disorder is a choice, not a disease."

☐ "Good families don't have problems like this."

☐ "They just need more willpower."

☐ Other belief I have held: ______________________________

Part 2: Reflection Questions

Where did these beliefs come from? (Family of origin? Community? Religion? Media?)

How did these beliefs shape the way you responded to your loved one's gambling?

Now that you have read Section 1.1, what belief about gambling have you reconsidered?

Module 1 Summary

Gambling disorder is a clinically recognized behavioral addiction driven by neurological changes in the brain's reward system. It is not a moral failing, a character weakness, or a choice — and it does not live in one person. It affects entire family systems, assigning roles and creating ripple effects of financial, emotional, physical, and relational harm. Understanding the disorder is the first step toward healing from it.

Before You Move On:

Module 2 invites you to turn the lens toward yourself — to honestly assess how living with a gambling problem has affected your own health, emotions, and well-being. Your experience matters, and naming it clearly is a powerful act of self-respect. When you are ready, turn to Module 2.

Module 2

Self-Assessment — Naming Your Experience

Clinical Rationale: Family members of people with gambling disorder frequently minimize and dismiss their own suffering. They become so focused on the gambler — monitoring their behavior, managing consequences, trying to prevent the next crisis — that they lose touch with what is happening to themselves. This module creates the space and structure to honestly assess the impact gambling has had on your emotional health, physical well-being, finances, and relationships. You cannot address what you have not named.

What You Will Gain from This Module

- Understanding of the secondary impacts of gambling disorder on family members
- A comprehensive four-domain impact inventory to name your experience concretely
- A stress and coping self-assessment with score interpretation
- A free narrative writing space to tell your story in your own words

2.1 How Has Gambling Affected Me?

Research on the families of problem gamblers consistently documents significant secondary harm — harm that is real, measurable, and clinically significant even though you are not the one who gambled. Studies indicate that partners and family members of problem gamblers experience rates of depression, anxiety, and stress-related illness comparable to those of the gamblers themselves. You have been carrying a weight that most people around you cannot see and do not understand.

The impacts typically fall across four interconnected domains:

- **Emotional:** Chronic anxiety, depression, rage, grief, shame, hopelessness, emotional numbness
- **Physical:** Sleep disturbance, headaches, gastrointestinal symptoms, fatigue, neglect of health care
- **Financial:** Debt, depleted savings, credit damage, income loss, inability to plan for the future
- **Relational:** Erosion of trust, social isolation, estrangement from friends and extended family, sexual intimacy problems, parenting challenges

2.2 The Hidden Toll: Emotional, Physical, Financial, and Relational Impact Inventory

---

WORKSHEET 2.2 — The Hidden Toll: Impact Inventory

Instructions: Read each item carefully. Check the box if you have experienced this, and use the "Notes" column to add any personal details that feel important. Be honest — this is for your own awareness and healing.

Domain 1: Emotional Impact

☐	Experience	My Notes
☐	Persistent anxiety or worry about money, the gambler's behavior, or the future	
☐	Depression, sadness, or feelings of hopelessness	
☐	Intense anger or rage — at the gambler, at yourself, at the situation	
☐	Emotional numbness or feeling "disconnected" from your feelings	

☐	Experience	My Notes
☐	Shame or embarrassment about your family situation	
☐	Guilt — feeling responsible for the gambler's behavior or for not stopping it sooner	
☐	Loss of joy in activities you used to enjoy	
☐	Constant vigilance — monitoring the gambler, checking bank accounts, scanning for signs	
☐	Feeling alone or like no one understands your situation	
☐	Loss of trust in your own judgment or perceptions	

Domain 2: Physical Impact

☐	Experience	My Notes
☐	Difficulty falling or staying asleep; waking in the night with worry	
☐	Chronic fatigue or exhaustion despite rest	
☐	Headaches, migraines, or tension in the body	
☐	Gastrointestinal problems (nausea, stomach pain, irritable bowel)	
☐	Changes in appetite — eating significantly more or less than usual	
☐	Neglecting routine medical or dental care due to stress or financial constraints	
☐	Using alcohol, food, or other substances to cope with stress	
☐	Increased smoking or caffeine use	
☐	Cardiovascular symptoms (palpitations, elevated blood pressure)	
☐	Overall decline in physical self-care and health maintenance	

Domain 3: Financial Impact

☐	Experience	My Notes
☐	Discovered debts you did not know about	
☐	Paid off debts created by the gambler's behavior	
☐	Depleted savings, retirement accounts, or investments	
☐	Damage to your personal credit score	
☐	Inability to meet regular household bills or expenses	
☐	Legal or collection actions related to gambling debts	
☐	Had to borrow money from family or friends to cover household needs	
☐	Unable to save for the future, children's education, or retirement	
☐	Fear or anxiety every time you check your bank account	
☐	Had property, assets, or valuables lost or sold due to gambling	

Domain 4: Relational Impact

☐	Experience	My Notes
☐	Loss of trust in the gambler — feeling unable to believe what they say	
☐	Withdrawal from friends, family, or social activities	
☐	Keeping the gambling problem secret from others to protect the gambler or the family	
☐	Conflict, arguments, or estrangement within the family	
☐	Breakdown of sexual intimacy or physical affection in the relationship	
☐	Feeling emotionally disconnected from the gambler	
☐	Impact on parenting — less present or effective as a parent due to stress	

☐	Experience	My Notes
☐	Children exhibiting behavioral or emotional problems	
☐	Considered or initiated separation or divorce	
☐	Lost friendships or family relationships because of the gambling situation	

Total Items Checked: ______ / 40

Looking at the domains where you checked the most items, what area of your life has been most affected?

2.3 My Stress and Coping Assessment

WORKSHEET 2.3 — My Stress and Coping Assessment

Instructions: For each item below, circle the number that best describes your experience *over the past two weeks*. Use the following scale:

1 = Almost Never | 2 = Rarely | 3 = Sometimes | 4 = Often | 5 = Almost Always

Statement	1	2	3	4	5
I feel overwhelmed by stress in my daily life.	1	2	3	4	5
I am getting adequate, restful sleep.	1	2	3	4	5
My mood is generally stable and manageable.	1	2	3	4	5
I feel physically healthy and am caring for my body.	1	2	3	4	5
I feel connected to supportive people in my life.	1	2	3	4	5
I am engaging in activities I enjoy or find meaningful.	1	2	3	4	5

Statement	1	2	3	4	5
I feel in control of my own decisions and choices.	1	2	3	4	5
I am able to set limits around my time and energy.	1	2	3	4	5
I feel hopeful about the future.	1	2	3	4	5
I take care of my own needs as well as the needs of others.	1	2	3	4	5

My Total Score: ______ / 50

Score Range	What It May Suggest
40–50	You are maintaining relatively strong coping. Continue your current practices and build on them.
28–39	Moderate stress and coping challenges. You are managing, but your reserves are being depleted. Targeted self-care is important now.
15–27	Significant stress and reduced coping capacity. Your well-being is substantially impacted. Consider reaching out for professional support.
10–14	High distress and very limited coping resources. Please connect with a therapist, counselor, or support group as soon as possible.

> **Clinical Note to Clinicians**
>
> *Scores in the 10–14 range should prompt a direct assessment of safety, suicidality, domestic violence risk, and co-occurring mental health conditions. Do not treat a low score on this assessment as a simple educational finding.*

What area of coping do you most want to strengthen?

____

2.4 Reflection Exercise: My Story in My Own Words

Reflection Exercise 2.4 — My Story in My Own Words

In the space below, write freely about your experience living with or loving someone with a gambling problem. There are no right or wrong answers, no grammar rules, no expectations. This is your space — honest, private, and entirely your own.

You might begin with: "It started when..." or "What no one understands is..." or simply with whatever rises first.

Module 2 Summary

Living with a gambling problem takes a measurable toll on your emotional health, physical well-being, financial stability, and relationships. Naming that impact is not complaining — it is the essential first step toward healing. The assessments in this module give you a clear picture of where you are right now, which is the only place any journey can begin.

Before You Move On:

Module 3 examines one of the most powerful and painful dynamics in families of gamblers: codependency and enabling. Understanding these patterns is not about blame — it is about freedom. When you are ready, continue to Module 3.

Module 3

Understanding Codependency and Enabling

Clinical Rationale: Codependency and enabling are among the most misunderstood and stigmatized concepts in addiction family work. Family members who enable a gambler are not weak, foolish, or complicit in the addiction — they are people who love someone deeply and who have been doing the best they could with the information and resources they had. This module explores these patterns with compassion, examines their roots in fear and love, and introduces evidence-based tools to begin shifting them.

What You Will Gain from This Module

- A clear, non-shaming clinical definition of codependency and how it develops
- Understanding of the difference between helping and enabling — and why enabling feels like love
- A comprehensive enabling inventory specific to gambling-affected families
- CBT thought record tools for identifying and restructuring enabling-driven automatic thoughts
- A comparison framework for distinguishing healthy helping from harmful enabling

3.1 What Is Codependency?

Codependency is a pattern of excessive emotional or behavioral focus on another person's needs, problems, or addictions — often at the cost of one's own well-being, identity, and autonomy. It is sometimes described as "losing yourself in someone else's story." In families affected by addiction, codependency typically develops gradually — not because the family member is flawed, but because they have been living in a system that has required it of them.

> **Definition: Codependency**
>
> A pattern of behaviors and beliefs in which one person's emotional functioning becomes excessively organized around managing, fixing, or accommodating another person's problematic behavior — at the expense of one's own needs, well-being, and sense of self.

Codependency in gambling-affected families often manifests as:

- Taking responsibility for solving the gambler's problems
- Feeling responsible for the gambler's emotional state
- Difficulty identifying what *you* want or feel, independent of the gambler's needs
- Deriving your sense of worth from being needed or from "saving" the gambler
- Suppressing your own feelings to avoid conflict or upsetting the gambler
- Believing that if you just did the right thing, found the right words, or loved enough — the gambling would stop

Codependency does not mean you are addicted to the gambler in a simplistic sense. It means the addiction has colonized the relational space so thoroughly that your own inner life has been crowded out. Recovery from codependency is not about caring less — it is about reclaiming your own life as equally important and equally real.

3.2 The Enabling Trap

Enabling is any behavior by a family member that shields the gambler from experiencing the natural consequences of their gambling — and in doing so, inadvertently removes one of the most powerful motivators for change. Enabling behaviors feel like help, but they function as fuel for the addiction cycle.

It is critical to understand: **enabling is almost never intentional.** Family members enable because they love, because they fear, because they are desperate, and because each individual enabling behavior made a certain kind of sense at the time. Understanding enabling is not about assigning blame — it is about recognizing patterns that have not produced the change you hoped for.

Common Enabling Behaviors in Gambling-Affected Families

- Paying off gambling debts to prevent financial collapse
- Making excuses for the gambler to employers, family members, or creditors
- Covering for the gambler when they miss commitments or appointments
- Providing money "for groceries" or "for rent" that is actually available to gamble
- Issuing ultimatums that are not followed through
- Keeping the gambling secret from others who could provide natural consequences
- Minimizing the severity of the problem to yourself or others
- Accepting apologies and promises without changed behavior

3.3 Worksheet: Am I Enabling? — The Enabling Inventory

WORKSHEET 3.3 — The Enabling Inventory

Clinical Note to Therapist

This inventory is designed to increase the client's awareness of enabling patterns specific to gambling disorder. It is not a diagnostic tool and should not be used to shame or blame. Process the results in session using Motivational Interviewing — explore ambivalence with compassion. Scoring is provided as a reflective aid, not a clinical measure.

Instructions: Read each behavior below carefully. For each one, place a checkmark (✓) in the column that best reflects how often you have engaged in this behavior. Be as honest as you can — there are no right or wrong answers. This is a tool for insight, not judgment.

Rating Scale:

Never – I have not done this
Sometimes – I have done this occasionally (1-3 times)
Often – I do this regularly
Always — This is my consistent pattern

Section A: Financial Enabling

Enabling Behavior	☐ Never	☐ Sometimes	☐ Often	☐ Always
1. I have paid gambling debts on behalf of my loved one.				
2. I have given my loved one money knowing they might gamble with it.				
3. I have bailed my loved one out of a financial crisis caused by gambling.				
4. I have taken over the gambler's financial responsibilities (bills, rent, loans) to prevent household collapse.				
5. I have sacrificed my own financial needs or savings to cover gambling-related losses.				

Enabling Behavior	☐ Never	☐ Sometimes	☐ Often	☐ Always
6. I have allowed my name to be used on accounts, loans, or credit to benefit the gambler.				
7. I have continued to share finances or joint accounts despite repeated dishonesty about money.				

Section B: Covering Up and Making Excuses

Enabling Behavior	☐ Never	☐ Sometimes	☐ Often	☐ Always
8. I have made excuses for my loved one's absences, broken promises, or missed events.				
9. I have lied to family members, friends, employers, or creditors to protect the gambler.				
10. I have kept the gambling a secret from people who could help.				
11. I have minimized or rationalized the gambling to myself (*"It's not that bad," "Everyone gambles," "They'll stop on their own"*).				
12. I have convinced others to forgive the gambler or give them another chance.				

Section C: Conflict Avoidance and Compliance

Enabling Behavior	☐ Never	☐ Sometimes	☐ Often	☐ Always
13. I have avoided raising the topic of gambling to keep the peace.				
14. I have accepted an apology and a promise to stop without seeing any real follow-through.				
15. I have issued a threat or ultimatum I did not follow through on.				

Enabling Behavior	☐ Never	☐ Sometimes	☐ Often	☐ Always
16. I have stayed silent when I knew gambling was occurring to avoid a confrontation.				
17. I have walked on eggshells around my loved one's mood to prevent a gambling episode.				

Section D: Caretaking and Rescuing

Enabling Behavior	☐ Never	☐ Sometimes	☐ Often	☐ Always
18. I have researched, monitored, or attempted to control my loved one's finances, devices, or location to prevent gambling.				
19. I have rewarded the gambler for not gambling (money, gifts, special treatment).				
20. I have provided transportation to a gambling venue or made gambling more accessible.				
21. I have provided housing, food, or basic needs to someone who continues to gamble despite agreeing to stop.				
22. I have bailed the gambler out of a legal situation (arrests, warrants, legal fees) caused by gambling.				

Section E: Emotional Enabling

Enabling Behavior	☐ Never	☐ Sometimes	☐ Often	☐ Always
23. I have used emotional appeals, guilt, or tears to try to motivate my loved one to stop gambling.				
24. I have blamed myself for the gambling — believing it is my fault or that I could have prevented it.				

Enabling Behavior	☐ Never	☐ Sometimes	☐ Often	☐ Always
25. I have suppressed my own anger, hurt, or needs to focus entirely on the gambler's wellbeing.				

Scoring Guide

Count the number of items checked **"Often"** or **"Always"**:

Score	What It May Indicate
0–3	Low enabling pattern — You have maintained some protective boundaries, though awareness is valuable.
4–8	Moderate enabling pattern — Some significant enabling behaviors are present. Review Section A most carefully.
9–15	High enabling pattern — Enabling is a central feature of this relationship. This workbook's boundary and communication modules will be especially important for you.
16–25	Pervasive enabling pattern — Enabling may feel completely normal or even necessary. Please know: this is a common response to living with addiction, and recovery is possible for you too.

> Remember:
>
> *Enabling behaviors develop out of love, fear, and survival — not weakness.*
>
> *Recognizing them is the first and most courageous step toward change.*

Post-Worksheet Reflection Questions

Take your time with the following questions. Write in full sentences if you can.

1. Which enabling behaviors have you engaged in most frequently?

2. What did you hope these behaviors would accomplish?

3. Have those behaviors produced the change you hoped for? Why or why not?

4. Which behavior on this list was hardest for you to acknowledge? What does that tell you?

5. If a close friend came to you describing doing these same things for a loved one who gambled, what would you say to them?

> Transition Prompt:
>
> *Before moving to Section 3.4, take a moment to breathe. Reviewing these patterns takes real courage. Whatever you discovered, you are already doing the most important thing: looking clearly at your situation so that things can change.*

3.4 Breaking Free from the Enabling Cycle — CBT Thought Patterns

---

Every enabling behavior begins with a thought — an automatic, often unconscious belief that makes enabling seem like the logical or loving choice. Cognitive Behavioral Therapy (CBT) helps us identify these automatic thoughts and examine whether they are accurate and whether acting on them is actually producing what we want.

The Thought Record

Instructions: Use the thought record below to examine a recent enabling situation. Fill in each column honestly. An example is provided in the first row.

WORKSHEET 3.4 — CBT Thought Record: Enabling Patterns

Situation	Automatic Thought	Emotion (Rate 0–100%)	Alternative Thought	New Behavior I Could Choose
Example: Gambler asked me for $200 for "groceries"	*"If I don't give it to them, the children won't eat."*	*Fear (85%), Guilt (70%)*	*"I can buy groceries myself and put them in the house without giving cash."*	*Go to the store myself, buy food directly.*

3.5 Reflection Exercise: What Fear Drives My Enabling?

Reflection Exercise 3.5 — The Fear Beneath the Enabling

Enabling is almost always driven by fear — not weakness, not stupidity, and not indifference to the consequences. Understanding which specific fear is driving your enabling is essential to beginning to shift it.

Check any fears that feel true for you:

☐ Fear that if I stop enabling, the gambler will leave me

☐ Fear that if I stop enabling, the gambler will hurt themselves

☐ Fear of conflict, anger, or retaliation

☐ Fear of financial collapse if I stop covering the debts

☐ Fear that I will be seen as a bad partner or parent

☐ Fear that I am giving up on someone I love

☐ Fear that stopping will make things worse before they get better

☐ Fear that I don't have the strength to hold a firm position

☐ Other: ______________________________

Describe the fear that most drives your enabling behavior in your own words:

What is the worst thing you imagine would happen if you stopped enabling?

How likely is that outcome, realistically? What evidence supports or challenges it?

3.6 Healthy Helping vs. Harmful Enabling

The distinction between helping and enabling is not always obvious. The table below offers a practical comparison, followed by a decision-making framework informed by the CRAFT model.

Healthy Helping	Harmful Enabling
Buying groceries and putting them in the house	Giving cash that may be used for gambling
Driving the gambler to a treatment appointment	Covering for missed work appointments caused by gambling
Expressing concern clearly, once, with specific examples	Repeated emotional pleading, threats, or ultimatums not followed through
Connecting the gambler with resources (hotlines, treatment options)	Making calls on the gambler's behalf that they could make themselves
Allowing natural consequences to occur	Paying off debts to protect the gambler from consequences
Maintaining your own emotional boundaries in conversation	Taking responsibility for managing the gambler's emotional state

Healthy Helping	Harmful Enabling
Seeking support for yourself through therapy or Gam-Anon	Focusing all energy on monitoring and controlling the gambler's behavior

CRAFT Approach Note

The Community Reinforcement and Family Training (CRAFT) model distinguishes between behaviors that reinforce gambling (enabling) and behaviors that reinforce non-gambling (healthy helping). CRAFT teaches family members to reward sober behavior warmly and consistently, and to disengage from reinforcing gambling behavior — not punitively, but strategically and compassionately.

Module 3 Summary

Codependency and enabling are understandable responses to the chaos of living with a gambling problem. They are driven by love, fear, and the desperate hope that the right move will finally make things change. But these patterns, however well-intentioned, often sustain the very cycle they seek to interrupt. With awareness, compassion, and tools, it is possible to shift from enabling to healthy helping — not all at once, and not without support, but gradually and powerfully.

Before You Move On:

Module 4 creates space for the emotional experience you may have been pushing aside in order to manage everyone else's. Grief, anger, shame, and guilt are the emotional landscape of this experience — and they deserve your full attention. Continue when you are ready.

Module 4

The Emotional Landscape — Grief, Anger, Shame, and Guilt

Clinical Rationale: Family members of gambling addicts carry an enormous emotional burden — one that is often invisible, disenfranchised, and actively suppressed in the service of managing the crisis. This module creates explicit, structured space to honor the emotional reality of living with or loving a problem gambler. Processing grief, anger, shame, and guilt is not self-indulgent — it is the clinical foundation for genuine recovery and relational healing.

What You Will Gain from This Module

- A framework for understanding grief in the context of a living loss
- Tools for processing anger and resentment in healthy, constructive ways
- Psychoeducation on shame and stigma and how they keep families isolated
- A comprehensive emotional inventory to map your current emotional experience
- A grief letter exercise and a CBT-based exercise for releasing guilt and self-blame

4.1 The Grief of Loving a Gambler

When we think of grief, we typically think of death. But grief is any response to significant loss — and families of gamblers experience a profound form of loss that is particularly painful precisely because it is ambiguous: the person they love is still physically present, yet the relationship they had — or hoped to have — has been fundamentally altered by the addiction.

This is called **disenfranchised grief** — grief that is not acknowledged, validated, or supported by society because it does not fit the traditional narrative of loss. There is no funeral for the relationship that gambling is destroying. There is no social permission to grieve someone who is still alive and standing in your kitchen.

The Stages of Grief Adapted to the Gambling Experience

Stage	What It Looks Like for Families of Gamblers
Denial	"It's not that serious." "They'll stop on their own." "Every family has problems like this."
Anger	Rage at the gambler for lying, for the financial damage, for breaking promises. Sometimes displaced onto children, employers, or self.
Bargaining	"If I cover this one last debt..." "If I'm a better partner, they'll stop." "Maybe if I just gave them more support..."
Depression	Profound sadness, withdrawal, hopelessness, loss of pleasure, questioning whether things will ever change.
Acceptance	Acknowledging the reality of the addiction — not as defeat, but as clarity that becomes the foundation for a new kind of decision-making.

A Compassionate Note

Grief stages are not linear. You may move between them in a single day. You may have cycled through them dozens of times over the years of your loved one's gambling. There is no "right" way to grieve, and no timeline by which you should be "over it."

4.2 Anger and Resentment — Understanding and Processing

Anger is one of the most common — and most suppressed — emotions in families of gamblers. Many family members, particularly women and individuals from cultures that discourage emotional expression, have learned to swallow their anger, redirect it, or feel profoundly ashamed of it. This module validates anger as a **normal, appropriate, and important signal**.

Anger tells you that something important has been violated — a value, a boundary, a trust, a commitment. The problem is not the anger itself; the problem is what happens when anger is never processed: it becomes resentment. And resentment, left unaddressed, becomes a chronic poison in the relational system — corroding not just the relationship with the gambler but the family member's capacity for joy, trust, and connection with others.

Healthy Anger Processing Strategies

- **Name it:** "I am angry because ___________."
- **Write it:** Journal without self-censorship — say what you cannot yet say out loud.
- **Move it:** Physical exercise, walking, or any body-based release.
- **Share it safely:** With a therapist, a Gam-Anon sponsor, or a trusted friend — not with the gambler in an unstructured confrontation.
- **Distinguish righteous anger from destructive rage:** Anger is a message; rage is what happens when the message has been ignored for too long.

4.3 Shame and Stigma — The Silent Wounds

Shame is the painful belief that there is something fundamentally wrong with you — not just that you have done something bad, but that you *are* bad, defective, or unworthy. In gambling-affected families, shame operates at multiple levels:

- **The gambler's shame:** Profound self-loathing that often drives further gambling as escape
- **The family's shame:** The belief that having a gambling problem in the family means there is something wrong with the family — a failure of oversight, love, or character
- **Cultural shame:** Particularly acute in communities where family honor, privacy, and the appearance of normalcy are deeply valued

The critical distinction: Guilt says "I did something bad." Shame says "I am bad." Guilt, in appropriate doses, can motivate change. Shame almost always makes things worse — it paralyzes, isolates, and fuels the very dynamics it condemns.

> **Key Clinical Point — Shame and Secrecy**
>
> Shame thrives in secrecy. One of the most powerful antidotes to shame is *connection* — sharing your experience with a safe person who responds with empathy rather than judgment. This is one of the core healing mechanisms of Gam-Anon and other peer support programs.

4.4 Worksheet: My Emotional Inventory

WORKSHEET 4.4 — My Emotional Inventory

Instructions: Review the emotions listed below. Circle any emotion you are currently experiencing. For each emotion you circle, complete the three columns to the right.

Emotion	Intensity (1–10)	Where Do I Feel It in My Body?	What Tends to Trigger It?
Grief / Sadness			
Anger / Rage			
Fear / Anxiety			
Shame			
Guilt			

Emotion	Intensity (1–10)	Where Do I Feel It in My Body?	What Tends to Trigger It?
Hopelessness			
Resentment			
Loneliness / Isolation			
Numbness / Emptiness			
Confusion			
Love (conflicted)			
Exhaustion / Depletion			
Disgust			
Relief (when not gambling)			
Hope (cautious)			
Betrayal			
Powerlessness			
Humiliation			
Sadness for your children			
Pride (in your own resilience)			
Other: ______________			

Looking at your emotional inventory, what do you notice?

Which emotion is most urgent for you right now?

4.5 Grief Letter Exercise

Exercise 4.5 — The Grief Letter (Unsent)

This exercise invites you to write an unsent letter to *the person your loved one used to be* — or the person you hoped they would be — before gambling took over. This is not a letter to send. It is a private act of grieving the relationship you had or wanted, and of honoring what you have lost.

Suggested paragraph prompts:

- *Paragraph 1: "When I first fell in love with you (or when we were close), you were..."*
- *Paragraph 2: "What I have lost because of the gambling is..."*
- *Paragraph 3: "What I miss most is..."*
- *Paragraph 4: "What I want you to know about what this has cost me is..."*
- *Paragraph 5: "Despite everything, I still..."*
- *Closing: "What I am allowing myself to grieve today is..."*

4.6 Reflection Exercise: Releasing Guilt and Shame

Reflection Exercise 4.6 — Cognitive Restructuring: Guilt and Self-Blame

Instructions: Below are common guilt-laden thoughts that family members of gamblers frequently experience, along with a rational alternative response. Read each pair, then use the blank rows to write your own guilt thoughts and challenge them.

Guilty Thought

Rational Response

"If I had been a better partner, they wouldn't have needed to gamble."

Gambling disorder is a neurological condition. No partner causes it, and no partner can cure it by being "better."

"I should have seen the signs sooner."

Gambling addicts are often highly skilled at concealment. You responded to the information you had.

"I enabled it by paying those debts — it's my fault things are this bad."

Enabling happens because of love and fear, not because of failure. Knowing better now is not the same as being responsible then.

"I feel guilty for being angry at someone who is sick."

You can acknowledge someone's illness and still feel justifiably angry about how their behavior has harmed you. Both are true.

Your guilt thought: ______________________________

Your rational response: ______________________________

Your guilt thought: ______________________________

Your rational response: ______________________________

Module 4 Summary

Grief, anger, shame, and guilt are the emotional terrain of loving a gambler. These emotions are not weaknesses — they are honest responses to real losses and real harms. Processing them with honesty, self-compassion, and structure is not self-indulgence; it is the foundation of your healing and your capacity to make clear, grounded decisions about your life.

Before You Move On:

Module 5 examines the trauma that can develop from living in a gambling-dominated household — including Secondary PTSD, hypervigilance, and what happens when anxiety becomes a way of life. You will also find evidence-based grounding exercises to bring you back to safety. Continue when you are ready.

Module 5

Trauma, Hypervigilance, and Secondary PTSD

Clinical Rationale: Living with an active gambling disorder is a traumatic experience. The chronic unpredictability, deception, financial crises, and emotional volatility of gambling households create conditions that can produce genuine trauma responses — including symptoms that meet the clinical threshold for Post-Traumatic Stress Disorder (PTSD). Trauma-Informed Care requires that we name this reality clearly, validate it fully, and provide practical tools for nervous system regulation.

What You Will Gain from This Module

- Understanding of how living with active gambling can produce trauma symptoms
- Knowledge of Secondary Traumatic Stress and Compassion Fatigue
- A trauma symptom checklist to identify your own responses
- Three evidence-based grounding and regulation exercises
- A guided reflection on when and how your sense of safety was lost

5.1 When Love Becomes Trauma

Trauma is not defined by the event itself — it is defined by the impact on the nervous system. When the brain and body are repeatedly exposed to situations of threat, unpredictability, or helplessness, the nervous system undergoes lasting changes in how it processes safety and danger. This is precisely what happens in gambling households.

Secondary Traumatic Stress (STS) — sometimes called "compassion fatigue" or "vicarious trauma" — occurs when a person develops trauma symptoms as a result of close, prolonged exposure to another person's suffering or crisis. Research on gambling-affected family members documents rates of clinically significant trauma symptoms that are substantially higher than in the general population.

Common trauma-producing experiences for families of gamblers include:

- Discovering large, hidden debts or financial devastation
- Witnessing the gambler's lies, promises, and subsequent betrayals repeatedly over time
- Experiencing emotional volatility, rage, or intimidation from the gambler
- Living in constant financial uncertainty and fear
- Discovering that the gambler has stolen from you, your children, or others
- Witnessing the gambler's depression, suicidal statements, or self-destructive behavior
- Experiencing the shame of creditors, legal actions, or public financial exposure

5.2 Recognizing Your Trauma Responses

The nervous system has three primary responses to perceived threat. In gambling households, family members may find themselves cycling between all three:

Response	How It Shows Up	In the Gambling Context
Fight	Anger, confrontation, arguing, aggression	Explosive arguments with the gambler; confronting perceived threats aggressively
Flight	Avoidance, leaving situations, burying oneself in work	Staying away from home; immersing in work or caregiving to escape the reality
Freeze	Paralysis, inability to act, shutdown	Knowing something needs to change but being unable to take action
Fawn	People-pleasing, appeasing, prioritizing others' needs to avoid conflict	Covering for the gambler, managing their emotions, enabling to keep the peace

Hypervigilance — a state of chronic, heightened alertness in which the nervous system is perpetually scanning for danger — is one of the most common and debilitating symptoms experienced by family members. It develops as an adaptive response to an unpredictable environment. When you never know what crisis is coming next, the nervous system stops feeling safe "between" crises and remains in a permanent state of high alert. This is exhausting, and it can persist long after the gambling stops.

5.3 Worksheet: My Trauma Symptom Checklist

WORKSHEET 5.3 — Trauma Symptom Checklist

Instructions: Check any symptoms you have experienced in relation to your loved one's gambling. This checklist is for self-awareness and clinical conversation — it is not a formal diagnostic tool.

Re-Experiencing Symptoms

☐ Intrusive memories or mental images of gambling-related crises

☐ Nightmares or disturbing dreams related to the gambling situation

☐ Flashbacks — feeling as though a past crisis is happening again

☐ Intense emotional distress when reminded of specific gambling events

☐ Physical reactions (racing heart, sweating, nausea) when triggered by reminders

Avoidance Symptoms

☐ Avoiding thoughts, feelings, or conversations related to the gambling

☐ Avoiding places, people, or activities that remind you of gambling events

☐ Feeling emotionally distant or detached from those around you

☐ Loss of interest in activities you used to enjoy

☐ Feeling as though the future is uncertain or shortened

Negative Cognitions and Mood

☐ Persistent negative beliefs about yourself ("I am foolish, weak, unworthy")

☐ Persistent negative beliefs about the world ("No one can be trusted")

☐ Blaming yourself for the gambling or its consequences

☐ Persistent feelings of fear, horror, anger, guilt, or shame

☐ Feeling cut off from or unable to have positive emotional experiences

Hyperarousal Symptoms

☐ Being easily startled by sounds, movement, or unexpected events

☐ Chronic tension, restlessness, or feeling "on edge"

☐ Difficulty concentrating

☐ Sleep disturbance — difficulty falling or staying asleep

☐ Irritability or angry outbursts out of proportion to the immediate trigger

> **Clinical Note — Please Read**
>
> If you checked five or more symptoms across multiple categories, or if any of these symptoms are significantly interfering with your daily functioning, please discuss this with a licensed mental health professional. Trauma symptoms are highly treatable with appropriate support — but they rarely resolve on their own without intervention.

5.4 Grounding and Regulation Skills

When the nervous system is dysregulated — when you are in a state of hyperarousal, panic, or shutdown — no amount of cognitive processing or decision-making will be effective. The first step is always to return the nervous system to a window of tolerance. The three exercises below are evidence-based tools you can use anywhere, anytime.

EXERCISE 5.4A — The 5-4-3-2-1 Sensory Grounding Technique

This exercise uses your five senses to anchor you in the present moment and interrupt a trauma response or anxiety spiral. It works because sensory experience is fundamentally present-moment — the senses do not exist in the past or future.

When you notice anxiety, hypervigilance, or a trauma response arising, pause and observe:

6. **5 things you can SEE** — Look around and name them. ______________________
7. **4 things you can TOUCH** — Feel your chair, your clothing, the air. ______________
8. **3 things you can HEAR** — Listen to the sounds in and around you. ______________
9. **2 things you can SMELL** — Notice any scent in your environment. ______________
10. **1 thing you can TASTE** — Notice any taste, or drink a sip of water. ______________

How do you feel after completing this exercise?

What situations will you use this technique for?

EXERCISE 5.4B — Box Breathing (4-4-4-4 Breathing)

Box breathing activates the parasympathetic nervous system — the "rest and digest" response — by deliberately regulating the breath. It is used by military personnel, first responders, and trauma therapists worldwide.

Instructions:

11. **Inhale** slowly through your nose for **4 counts**
12. **Hold** the breath for **4 counts**
13. **Exhale** slowly through your mouth for **4 counts**
14. **Hold** (lungs empty) for **4 counts**
15. Repeat **4–6 times**

Practice this technique right now before moving on. How does your body feel afterward?

When in your daily life could you build in this practice regularly?

EXERCISE 5.4C — Safe Place Visualization

This exercise creates a mental sanctuary — a place (real or imagined) where you feel completely safe, calm, and at ease. Your brain does not fully distinguish between vividly imagined experience and real experience, which is why visualization is a clinically effective regulation tool.

Instructions: Close your eyes and imagine a place where you feel completely safe and at peace. It may be a real place from your past, a place in nature, or a completely imagined space. Take 2–3 minutes to let the image develop.

Describe your safe place in detail below (what you see, hear, smell, feel):

Give your safe place a name so you can return to it quickly: ________________________________

Practice visiting this place in your mind for 5 minutes each day this week.

5.5 Reflection Exercise: When Did I Stop Feeling Safe?

Reflection Exercise 5.5 — The Moment Safety Shifted

There is often a specific moment — or a series of moments — when a family member realizes that their home no longer feels safe, predictable, or trustworthy. Identifying that moment is not about re-traumatizing yourself; it is about honoring the reality of what happened to you and understanding why your nervous system is doing what it is doing.

Describe the moment (or period) when you first realized something was seriously wrong:

How did your body respond in that moment?

How has your sense of safety in your home changed since then?

What would it take for your home or your life to feel safe again?

Module 5 Summary

Living with an active gambler can produce genuine trauma — not metaphorically, but neurologically and clinically. Your hypervigilance, intrusive thoughts, emotional numbing, and chronic anxiety are not character flaws; they are adaptive responses to an genuinely threatening environment. Recognizing them as trauma responses is the first step toward healing them. The grounding exercises in this module are tools you can use immediately and repeatedly to begin regulating your nervous system.

Before You Move On:

Module 6 addresses the financial devastation that gambling disorder so frequently causes — one of the most concrete and urgent dimensions of this experience. You will find assessment tools, safety planning, and a roadmap for financial recovery. Continue when you are ready.

Module 6

Financial Devastation and Recovery

Clinical Rationale: Financial harm is among the most immediate, concrete, and devastating consequences of gambling disorder for families. Unlike emotional wounds that can remain invisible, financial damage is measurable — and for many families, it represents the destruction of years or decades of accumulated security. This module addresses financial impact directly, with practical assessment tools, safety planning, and a recovery roadmap.

What You Will Gain from This Module

- A clear picture of the typical financial impact of gambling disorder on families
- A structured financial inventory to assess your current situation
- Concrete financial safety planning steps
- A short-, medium-, and long-term financial recovery goal-setting worksheet
- A reflective exercise on how this experience has changed your relationship with money

6.1 The Financial Impact of Gambling on Families

Research paints a sobering picture of the financial toll of gambling disorder. Studies indicate that the average debt accumulated by individuals with severe gambling disorder ranges from $40,000 to over $80,000, with many cases involving debt in the six figures. Bankruptcy filings, mortgage defaults, retirement account depletion, and fraudulent loan applications are all well-documented in the clinical literature on gambling disorder.

Common Financial Deceptions Used by Gamblers

- Opening secret credit cards or loan accounts without the family's knowledge
- Falsifying tax returns or pay stubs to obtain additional credit
- Withdrawing from joint retirement or savings accounts
- Borrowing from multiple family members and friends simultaneously
- Diverting direct deposit to a hidden account
- Selling household items, jewelry, or valuables
- Taking out second mortgages or home equity loans without disclosure
- Using children's savings, college funds, or custodial accounts
- Manipulating insurance claims or committing financial fraud

Important: Financial Fraud and Legal Exposure

In some cases, gambling-related financial deception may rise to the level of fraud, identity theft, or other criminal activity. If you have discovered that your identity, credit, or accounts have been used without your consent, consult with both a financial counselor and a legal professional as soon as possible. You may have legal protections and remedies available to you.

6.2 Assessing Your Financial Damage — The Family Financial Inventory

One of the most disorienting aspects of loving someone with a gambling disorder is the financial fog that develops over time. Money disappears without explanation. Accounts are overdrawn. Loans appear on credit reports you never authorized. Before you can chart a path forward, you need to see clearly where you stand. This inventory is not about blame — it is about clarity. Financial clarity is one of the most empowering first steps in your recovery as a family member.

Complete this worksheet as honestly as you can. If you do not know exact figures, write your best estimate and mark it with a "?" so you can verify later. If possible, bring supporting documents (bank statements, credit reports, loan paperwork) to this exercise.

> **Clinical Note to Therapist**
> This inventory may surface significant distress, shame, or overwhelm. Introduce it with psychoeducation about financial trauma and normalize difficulty completing it. Consider breaking it into two sessions if needed. A referral to a nonprofit credit counselor or financial social worker is strongly encouraged for clients with complex financial damage. Remind clients: this is data, not a verdict.

PART 1: ASSETS — WHAT YOU HAVE

Instructions: List your current assets. Include only what is in your name or jointly held. Mark joint accounts with (J) and accounts solely in your name with (M).

Asset Type	Estimated Value	Notes
Checking account(s)	$ ________	
Savings account(s)	$ ________	
Retirement account (401k, IRA, pension)	$ ________	
Investment accounts	$ ________	
Home / real estate equity	$ ________	
Vehicle(s) — current market value	$ ________	
Other valuable property (jewelry, equipment, etc.)	$ ________	
Other: ____________	$ ________	
TOTAL ESTIMATED ASSETS	$ ________	

PART 2: LIABILITIES — WHAT YOU OWE

Instructions: List all debts, including any you recently discovered. Mark debts the gambler took out in your name or jointly without your full knowledge with an asterisk (*).

Debt Type	Creditor / Lender	Amount Owed	In Whose Name?
Mortgage / rent arrears	________	$ ________	________
Car loan(s)	________	$ ________	________
Credit card #1	________	$ ________	________
Credit card #2	________	$ ________	________
Credit card #3	________	$ ________	________
Personal loan(s)	________	$ ________	________
Payday / cash advance loan(s)	________	$ ________	________
Loan from family or friends	________	$ ________	________
Medical bills	________	$ ________	________
Tax debt / IRS	________	$ ________	________
Gambling-related debt (bookies, apps, casino markers)	________	$ ________	________
Legal fees / court costs related to gambling	________	$ ________	________
Other: ____________	________	$ ________	________
Other: ____________	________	$ ________	________
TOTAL ESTIMATED LIABILITIES		$ ________	

NET FINANCIAL POSITION (Assets minus Liabilities): $ ____________

PART 3: MONTHLY CASH FLOW SNAPSHOT

Instructions: Estimate your current monthly income and expenses to understand your ongoing financial gap.

MONTHLY INCOME

Income Source	Monthly Amount
My employment income (take-home)	$ ________
Partner/spouse income (if applicable)	$ ________
Child support / alimony received	$ ________
Government assistance / disability	$ ________
Other income: ________	$ ________
TOTAL MONTHLY INCOME	$ ________

MONTHLY ESSENTIAL EXPENSES

Expense	Monthly Amount
Rent / mortgage	$ ________
Utilities (electric, gas, water)	$ ________
Groceries / household supplies	$ ________
Transportation (car payment, gas, insurance, transit)	$ ________
Health insurance / medical costs	$ ________
Child care / school expenses	$ ________
Minimum debt payments	$ ________
Phone / internet	$ ________
Other essential: ________	$ ________
TOTAL MONTHLY EXPENSES	$ ________

MONTHLY CASH FLOW GAP (Income minus Expenses): $ ________

What Your Gap Tells You
A negative number here means you are currently spending more than you earn — a common reality for families of gamblers. This is not a permanent state. The Financial Safety Planning section (6.3) and the Financial Recovery Roadmap worksheet (6.4) will help you begin building a path forward. If your gap is severe, please prioritize a consultation with a nonprofit credit counselor (see Appendix A for resources).

PART 4: FINANCIAL DECEPTION INVENTORY

Instructions: Check all that apply. This section helps identify the scope of financial dishonesty that has occurred. It is important information, not an accusation.

☐ I discovered accounts, loans, or credit cards I did not know existed
☐ Money was taken from our joint account without my knowledge or consent
☐ My credit was used without my explicit permission
☐ My identity or personal information was used to obtain credit or cash
☐ Assets (home equity, retirement funds, savings) were accessed or depleted without my knowledge
☐ The gambler forged my signature or impersonated me financially
☐ Tax returns were withheld, falsified, or filed fraudulently
☐ Family members or friends were borrowed from without my knowledge
☐ I discovered gambling-related debt only after a crisis (collections, lawsuit, foreclosure notice)
☐ I was deliberately kept off financial accounts or excluded from financial decisions
☐ Other: ________________________________

Total items checked: ________

⚠ Important Safety Note
If you checked items involving identity theft, forgery, or unauthorized use of credit, you may have legal options beyond financial recovery. An attorney specializing in family financial fraud, a credit bureau fraud alert, or a consultation with your state's consumer protection office may be appropriate next steps. Document everything you discover.

PART 5: CREDIT IMPACT ASSESSMENT

Current credit score (if known): ________ (Free report available at AnnualCreditReport.com)
Have you reviewed your credit report in the last 90 days? ☐ Yes ☐ No

Item Found on Credit Report	Amount	Authorized by Me?
________________________	$ ________	☐ Yes ☐ No
________________________	$ ________	☐ Yes ☐ No
________________________	$ ________	☐ Yes ☐ No
________________________	$ ________	☐ Yes ☐ No

PART 6: REFLECTION QUESTIONS

Take your time with these questions. Financial trauma is real. You do not have to solve everything today — you just need to see it clearly.

1. **What was the most difficult part of completing this inventory?**

____

____

____

2. **What financial information surprised or shocked you most?**

____

____

____

3. **Before completing this inventory, were you aware of the full scope of the financial damage? What kept you from seeing it clearly?**

____

____

____

4. **What is the single most urgent financial issue you need to address in the next 30 days?**

____

____

____

5. **What financial goal — however small — feels achievable right now?**

____

____

____

Closing Encouragement

Completing this inventory is an act of courage. Many family members have avoided this step for months or years out of fear, shame, or overwhelm. By facing these numbers, you have taken the most important step: you know where you stand. From here, we can build forward together. Move to Section 6.3: Financial Safety Planning when you are ready.

6.3 Financial Safety Planning

Financial safety planning is the process of taking concrete steps to protect your financial well-being from further damage. The following action steps are not punitive — they are practical measures of self-protection. Check off each step as you complete it, and add a target date.

WORKSHEET 6.3 — Financial Safety Planning Checklist

☐	Action Step	Target Date	Completed
☐	Pull your credit report from all three bureaus (Equifax, Experian, TransUnion) at AnnualCreditReport.com	____________	☐
☐	Place a credit freeze on your individual accounts to prevent new accounts being opened in your name	____________	☐
☐	Open an individual bank account in your name only at a different institution	____________	☐
☐	Redirect your direct deposit or income to your individual account	____________	☐
☐	Consult with a non-profit financial counselor (NFCC member agency)	____________	☐
☐	Consult with a family law attorney about financial liability for a spouse's debts	____________	☐
☐	Identify and secure any accounts the gambler has access to that hold your assets	____________	☐
☐	Review and update beneficiary designations on insurance, retirement, and estate documents	____________	☐
☐	Create a list of all known accounts, loans, and financial obligations	____________	☐
☐	Consult with a bankruptcy attorney if debt is unmanageable (free initial consultations are widely available)	____________	☐

6.4 Worksheet: My Financial Recovery Roadmap

WORKSHEET 6.4 — My Financial Recovery Roadmap

Time Frame	Financial Goal	Action Steps	Support Needed
30 Days *(Immediate stability)*			
6 Months *(Building safety)*			
1 Year *(Longer-term recovery)*			

The one financial step I will take this week is:

6.5 Reflection Exercise: My Relationship with Money After Gambling

---

Reflection Exercise 6.5 — Money, Trust, and Security

How has the gambling experience changed the way you think and feel about money?

What does financial security mean to you now, compared to before this experience began?

What has this experience taught you about trust — financial and otherwise?

What is one thing you want to reclaim in your financial life?

Module 6 Summary

Financial devastation is one of the most concrete and urgent harms caused by gambling disorder. Taking stock of your situation clearly — without shame, without minimization — is the first step toward reclaiming your financial future. Financial recovery is possible, and it begins with one practical step at a time.

Before You Move On:

Module 7 addresses one of the most powerful tools available to you: the ability to set and hold boundaries. Boundaries are not punishments — they are acts of self-respect that create the conditions for genuine change. Continue when you are ready.

Module 7

Setting Boundaries — Protecting Yourself Without Punishing Them

Clinical Rationale: Boundary-setting is consistently identified in both clinical practice and empirical research as one of the most critical and most difficult skills for family members of addicts to develop. In the context of gambling addiction, where financial entanglement, emotional enmeshment, and chronic crisis are the norm, boundaries are not optional — they are the foundation of self-protection, recovery, and potentially the most effective motivational leverage for the gambler's own change process.

What You Will Gain from This Module

- A clear clinical definition of boundaries and why they are acts of love, not punishment
- Specific boundary examples for spouses/partners and for parents of adult gamblers
- A comprehensive four-domain Boundary Blueprint worksheet
- The CRAFT LOVE MAP communication model for stating a boundary effectively
- Strategies for holding boundaries when they are tested or violated

7.1 What Are Boundaries?

A boundary is a clear, specific statement of what you will and will not accept in a relationship — and what you will do if that limit is violated. Boundaries are not walls designed to keep others out; they are fences with gates that you control. They communicate your values, protect your well-being, and create the structural conditions within which healthy relationships can exist.

Boundaries vs. Ultimatums

An **ultimatum** is a threat issued in the heat of emotion, often without a genuine intention to follow through. A **boundary** is a calm, consistent, pre-determined response to a specific behavior — one that you are fully prepared to uphold. The key difference is your own readiness and follow-through. Boundaries that are not enforced become ultimatums that teach the gambler that you do not mean what you say.

Boundaries in the context of gambling-affected families serve two simultaneous functions:

- **Self-protection:** They prevent you from continuing to absorb harm from the gambling behavior
- **Natural consequences:** By removing your buffer between the gambler and reality, they create the conditions under which the gambler may experience genuine motivation to change

7.2 Types of Boundaries for Families of Gamblers

For Spouses and Partners

Domain	Example Boundary
Financial	"I will no longer give you cash or access to joint accounts. I will pay household bills directly."
Financial	"If I discover another hidden debt, I will consult a divorce attorney."
Emotional	"I will not engage in arguments about gambling after 9 PM. I will leave the room."
Communication	"I will only discuss the gambling with you in the presence of our couples therapist."
Physical space	"If you come home under the influence of gambling (agitated, chaotic), I will take the children to my parents' home for the night."
Sexual/Intimacy	"I cannot be intimate with you while active lying and gambling are ongoing."

For Parents of Adult Gamblers

Domain	Example Boundary
Financial	"I will not give you money, loans, or pay your debts. If you need food, I will buy groceries."
Housing	"You may not live in this home if gambling continues. This is not negotiable."
Contact	"I will not answer calls in the middle of the night unless it is a genuine emergency."
Legal liability	"I will not co-sign any loan, act as a guarantor, or take any financial risk on your behalf."
Grandchildren	"You will not be alone with the grandchildren while actively gambling."

7.3 Worksheet: My Boundary Blueprint

WORKSHEET 7.3 — My Boundary Blueprint

Instructions: For each of the four domains below, complete the three prompts. Be specific — vague boundaries are easily blurred. Write only boundaries you are genuinely prepared to uphold.

Financial Boundaries

My current financial limit is:

The financial boundary I need to set is:

If this boundary is violated, I will:

My support for holding this boundary is:

Emotional Boundaries

My current emotional limit is:

The emotional boundary I need to set is:

If this boundary is violated, I will:

My support for holding this boundary is:

Physical / Space Boundaries

My current physical limit is:

The physical boundary I need to set is:

If this boundary is violated, I will:

My support for holding this boundary is:

Relational / Communication Boundaries

My current relational limit is:

The relational boundary I need to set is:

If this boundary is violated, I will:

My support for holding this boundary is:

7.4 How to Communicate a Boundary — The CRAFT LOVE MAP

The CRAFT model recommends a specific approach to communicating a boundary or making a behavioral request. The LOVE MAP approach helps you stay calm, specific, and grounded when stating your boundary — even in a charged emotional environment.

Letter	Component	What It Means	Example
L	Listen	Begin by acknowledging the other person's perspective, even briefly.	"I know this conversation is hard for you to hear."
O	Offer information	State the specific behavior you are addressing — factually, without blame labels.	"When money disappears from our account without explanation..."
V	Validate	Acknowledge the emotional reality — yours or theirs — without attacking.	"I feel frightened and unable to trust what I'm seeing."
E	Explain consequences	State clearly and calmly what you will do if the behavior continues — and mean it.	"Going forward, I will be managing our household finances separately."
M	Make a request	State what you are asking for specifically and behaviorally.	"I am asking you to agree to a joint session with a counselor this week."
A	Affirm the positive	Close with something genuine about the relationship or what you want for the future.	"I love you and I want us to find a way through this together."
P	Practice and prepare	Role-play the conversation before having it; prepare for emotional reactions.	Write it out; practice with your therapist or a trusted friend.

7.5 When Boundaries Are Violated — Holding the Line

The moment a boundary is tested is the moment it becomes real. Every time you state a boundary and do not follow through with the consequence, you teach the other person that your boundaries are not real. This is not a moral failure — it is an understandable human dynamic, especially when love, fear, and financial dependence are involved. But it is also the primary reason boundaries fail to produce change.

Strategies for holding boundaries when tested:

- **Prepare in advance:** Know exactly what you will do when the boundary is violated — have a plan, not just a principle.

- **Have a support person on call:** Someone who can help you stay grounded when you are tempted to relent.
- **Separate emotion from action:** You can feel sad, guilty, or conflicted AND follow through on the boundary. Both are true simultaneously.
- **Practice self-compassion when you slip:** A lapse in holding a boundary is not a failure — it is information. Return to it without self-attack.
- **Celebrate every time you hold it:** Holding a boundary is a courageous act. Notice it and acknowledge it.

7.6 Reflection Exercise: What Have I Been Afraid to Say?

Reflection Exercise 7.6 — The Boundaries I Have Needed All Along

What boundary have you known you needed to set but have been afraid to state?

What fear has stopped you from setting it?

What have the costs been — to you — of not setting this boundary?

What might life look like six months from now if this boundary were in place?

Module 7 Summary

Boundaries are not cruelty — they are clarity. They protect you from ongoing harm, communicate your values, and create the conditions under which genuine change becomes possible. Setting and holding boundaries in the context of gambling addiction is one of the most clinically effective and personally courageous things a family member can do.

Before You Move On:

Module 8 addresses communication — how gambling destroys it, how to reclaim it, and how to use evidence-based communication tools in even the most charged household environments. Continue when you are ready.

Module 8

Communication Strategies for Chaotic Households

Clinical Rationale: Communication in gambling-affected households is almost universally compromised — by deception, by emotional flooding, by the exhaustion of chronic crisis, and by the defensive dynamics that develop when honesty has repeatedly produced painful consequences. This module provides evidence-based communication tools to help family members express themselves clearly, manage conflict effectively, and begin restoring the possibility of genuine dialogue.

What You Will Gain from This Module

- Understanding of how gambling systematically erodes communication in families
- Training in the three communication styles and how to develop assertiveness
- A self-assessment of your current communication patterns
- The CRAFT model in practice for gambling-specific communication challenges
- Structured I-Statement practice with real gambling scenarios
- Preparation for the most important conversation you need to have

8.1 How Gambling Destroys Communication

Deception is the foundational communication injury in gambling relationships. When a family member discovers that they have been lied to — about money, about whereabouts, about the extent of gambling — a fundamental rupture in the communication system occurs. Trust, once broken repeatedly, becomes the lens through which every subsequent interaction is filtered: *Is this true? What is being hidden? What am I not seeing?*

Common destructive communication patterns in gambling households include:

- **Walking on eggshells:** Monitoring mood, suppressing honest communication to avoid triggering the gambler's defensiveness or anger
- **The pursuer-distancer dynamic:** One partner pursues for honesty and engagement; the other distances, withdraws, and stonewalls
- **Emotional flooding:** Conversations about gambling escalate quickly to overwhelming emotional intensity, making productive dialogue impossible
- **Stonewalling:** Complete emotional shutdown — physically present, emotionally unavailable
- **Contempt and criticism:** Chronic resentment expressed as attack on character rather than specific behavior

8.2 Assertive Communication Skills

Style	Description	Example Response
Passive	Suppresses own needs and feelings; avoids conflict; communicates indirectly or not at all	"It's fine... whatever you want."
Aggressive	Prioritizes own needs through attack, blame, or intimidation; communicates disrespect for others	"You're a liar and you don't care about anyone but yourself!"
Assertive	Expresses own needs and feelings clearly and respectfully; honors both self and other	"When money is missing without explanation, I feel frightened and unable to trust what I'm seeing. I need us to talk about this."

The I-Statement Formula

When __________ [specific behavior], I feel __________ [emotion], because __________ [impact]. I need/want __________ [specific request].

I-Statements focus on your experience rather than the other person's character — which reduces defensiveness and keeps conversation open.

De-escalation Techniques

- Use a calm, steady tone of voice — even when you do not feel calm
- Take a 20-minute break if emotional flooding is occurring (both parties' heart rates must return to baseline for effective communication)
- Use physical grounding (feel your feet on the floor, breathe slowly) during difficult conversations
- When the conversation is not productive, disengage clearly: "I want to continue this conversation, and I can't do it productively right now. Let's plan to talk tomorrow at 6 PM."

8.3 Worksheet: Communication Pattern Inventory

WORKSHEET 8.3 — Communication Pattern Inventory

Instructions: Rate each item using the following scale: 1 = Never | 2 = Rarely | 3 = Sometimes | 4 = Often | 5 = Almost Always

Statement	1	2	3	4	5
I say what I need clearly and directly, without hinting.	1	2	3	4	5
I suppress my feelings to avoid upsetting the gambler.	1	2	3	4	5

Statement	1	2	3	4	5
I raise my voice or become emotionally intense during arguments.	1	2	3	4	5
I shut down or go silent when conversations become too charged.	1	2	3	4	5
I rehearse what I want to say but never say it.	1	2	3	4	5
I take responsibility for keeping the peace in my household.	1	2	3	4	5
I make requests specifically rather than dropping hints.	1	2	3	4	5
I am able to disengage from an unproductive argument.	1	2	3	4	5
I attack the gambler's character rather than their specific behavior.	1	2	3	4	5
I feel heard and understood after conversations about the gambling.	1	2	3	4	5

Patterns I notice in my communication:

Communication patterns I learned in my family of origin that may be showing up now:

8.4 The CRAFT Communication Model in Practice

CRAFT's approach to communication with a person struggling with addiction is grounded in a specific set of principles: be specific rather than general, focus on behavior rather than character, make requests rather than demands, and choose the right moment to communicate (not during active gambling, not during an argument, not when either party is exhausted or intoxicated).

CRAFT Communication Principles for Gambling-Specific Situations

Instead of this...	Try this...
"You always lie to me. I can never trust you."	"When I discovered money was missing from our account without discussion, I felt frightened and betrayed. I need us to agree on a financial transparency arrangement."
"You're destroying this family. Stop gambling."	"I've seen how the gambling has affected our finances and our relationship. I want to talk about what help might look like when you're ready."
"If you loved me, you would stop."	"I love you, and I need you to know that continuing this way isn't something I can do long-term. I want things to be different between us."

8.5 Worksheet: Practicing the I-Statement

WORKSHEET 8.5 — I-Statement Practice

Instructions: For each scenario below, write an I-Statement using the formula: *When __ [behavior], I feel __ [emotion], because __ [impact]. I need/want __ [request].*

Example (completed for you):

Scenario: You discovered the gambler spent $800 you needed for rent.
I-Statement: *"When I discovered that $800 was spent on gambling when we needed it for rent, I felt frightened and furious, because I don't know how we will cover housing this month. I need us to immediately open a separate account for bill payment that only I control."*

Scenario 1: The gambler broke a promise to attend a child's school event because they were gambling.

My I-Statement:

Scenario 2: You discovered a credit card you didn't know about with a $6,000 balance.

My I-Statement:

Scenario 3: The gambler asked you for money, claiming it is for groceries.

My I-Statement:

Scenario 4: The gambler came home at 3 AM after saying they would be home by 10 PM.

My I-Statement:

Scenario 5: The gambler has promised to get help three times and has not followed through.

My I-Statement:

Scenario 6: The gambler denies that gambling is a problem despite clear evidence.

My I-Statement:

Scenario 7: You need to tell the gambler that you have sought your own counseling.

My I-Statement:

Scenario 8: (Write your own real situation here)

Situation:

My I-Statement:

8.6 Reflection Exercise: The Conversation I Need to Have

Reflection Exercise 8.6 — Planning the Most Important Conversation

What is the most important thing you have not yet said to your loved one about the gambling?

What has stopped you from saying it?

How might you open this conversation? Draft your opening sentence:

How do you anticipate they will respond? How will you prepare for that response?

What support do you need before having this conversation?

Module 8 Summary

Effective communication in the context of gambling addiction is a skill that can be learned and practiced, even in chaotic or emotionally charged environments. The CRAFT communication model, the I-Statement formula, and assertiveness training give you a framework for speaking your truth clearly, calmly, and in ways that maximize the possibility of being heard.

Before You Move On:

Module 9 turns attention to the children in the household — often the silent witnesses and the most vulnerable members of a gambling-affected family system. Continue when you are ready.

Module 9

Protecting Children in Gambling Households

Clinical Rationale: Children living in households where a parent or caregiver has a gambling problem are among the most vulnerable and least visible members of the gambling-affected family. They rarely receive direct attention or services, despite experiencing significant emotional, behavioral, and developmental harm. This module provides parents and caregivers with the knowledge, tools, and strategies needed to protect children and mitigate the impact of the gambling-disordered environment.

What You Will Gain from This Module

- Research-based understanding of how parental gambling affects children at different developmental stages
- Guidance on age-appropriate conversations with children about gambling
- A behavioral checklist to monitor children's well-being
- Practical strategies for creating stability and safety in a chaotic household
- A values-based reflection on what you want for your children's future

9.1 How Children Are Affected by a Parent's Gambling

Research on the children of problem gamblers consistently documents elevated rates of emotional and behavioral difficulties, including anxiety disorders, depression, conduct problems, academic underperformance, and social withdrawal. These children are also at significantly elevated risk of developing their own gambling problems in adulthood — a sobering finding that underscores the urgency of early intervention and family support.

The connection to **Adverse Childhood Experiences (ACEs)** is important here. ACE research demonstrates that growing up in a household characterized by chronic financial stress, parental dysfunction, emotional unavailability, and unpredictability has lasting effects on brain development, physical health, mental health, and life outcomes. Living with a gambling-disordered parent meets multiple ACE criteria.

Specific Impacts on Children in Gambling Households

- **Parentification:** Children who take on adult roles — managing household tasks, monitoring the gambler, or emotionally supporting the non-gambling parent — at the expense of their own development
- **Emotional neglect:** Parents preoccupied with financial crisis and the gambler's behavior often have little emotional bandwidth for children's needs
- **Exposure to conflict and tension:** Chronic household conflict is one of the most damaging environmental stressors for children's development
- **Financial shame:** Children may experience peer embarrassment, social exclusion, or academic impact related to the family's financial struggles
- **Modeling of risk behavior:** Normalized gambling in the household increases children's own gambling risk significantly

9.2 Age-Appropriate Conversations with Children About Gambling

Children need honest, developmentally appropriate information about what is happening in their family — and they need explicit permission to have their feelings about it. Silence, secrets, and minimization typically worsen children's distress rather than protect them from it.

Age Group	What to Say	What to Avoid
Toddlers and Preschool (2–5)	"Daddy/Mommy is sick and needs help from doctors. It's not your fault. We love you." Use simple, concrete language. Maintain routines.	Detailed explanations; adult financial information; putting them in the middle.
School-Age (6–11)	"Our family is going through a hard time because [parent] has a problem called a gambling addiction. It is a kind of sickness. It is not your fault, and your job is just to be a kid."	Blaming the gambler in front of the child; using the child as an emotional support; exposing them to adult arguments about finances.
Adolescents (12–18)	More direct explanation of addiction as a disorder; validate their anger, grief, and confusion; provide factual information; offer professional support; discuss the family's plans without making them responsible for the outcome.	Expecting them to manage their own emotions independently; placing adult responsibilities on them; dismissing their anger or resentment.

Key Message for All Children

Every child in a gambling-affected household needs to hear three things clearly and repeatedly: **(1) This is not your fault. (2) You are safe. (3) There are adults working on this problem.**

9.3 Worksheet: My Child's Behavioral Checklist

WORKSHEET 9.3 — Child Behavioral and Emotional Observation Checklist

Instructions: For each of your children, check any behaviors or emotional signs you have observed in the past 3 months. Note the child's approximate age next to their name.

Child's name/age: ____________________ Child's name/age: ____________________

☐	Observed Behavior or Sign	Child 1 Notes	Child 2 Notes
☐	Increased anxiety, worry, or fearfulness		
☐	Withdrawal from friends, activities, or family		
☐	Decline in academic performance or school attendance		
☐	Increased irritability, anger, or acting out		
☐	Sleep disturbances (nightmares, trouble falling asleep, bedwetting)		
☐	Somatic complaints (stomachaches, headaches) without medical cause		
☐	Taking on adult-level household responsibilities (parentification)		
☐	Asking questions about money, debt, or family finances		
☐	Expressing guilt or responsibility for the family's problems		
☐	Statements about hopelessness, not wanting to go to school, or not wanting to be here		
☐	Eating changes (significantly more or less than usual)		
☐	Increased interest in gambling, games of chance, or risk-taking		

Clinical Note — Child Safety

If a child has made any statements suggesting hopelessness or not wanting to be here, seek immediate assessment from a licensed child mental health professional or school counselor. If you are checking more than five items for any child, consultation with a child therapist is strongly recommended.

What have you noticed most about your child(ren) in recent months?

9.4 Creating Stability Amid Chaos — The Safe Harbor Plan

Even in the midst of an ongoing gambling crisis, there are practical steps you can take as a parent to create pockets of safety, predictability, and warmth for your children. Children are remarkably resilient when they have at least one stable, attuned adult in their lives who consistently shows up for them.

MY SAFE HARBOR PLAN — Creating Stability for My Children

Strategy	How I Will Implement This	Starting Date
Maintain consistent daily routines (meals, bedtime, school)		
Shield children from financial arguments and adult gambling conversations		
Have one-on-one time with each child weekly		
Identify at least one trusted adult outside the home for each child		
Connect children with a school counselor or child therapist		
Create a family check-in time where feelings are welcomed without judgment		
Ensure children have consistent access to extracurricular activities and peer connection		

9.5 Reflection Exercise: What Do I Want for My Children?

Reflection Exercise 9.5 — Your Vision for Your Children

What kind of childhood do you want your children to have?

What kind of home do you want them to grow up in?

How does the current situation conflict with that vision?

What is one concrete step you can take this week for your child(ren)?

Module 9 Summary

Children in gambling-affected households are vulnerable but resilient — especially when they have access to at least one attuned, stable adult. Your decision to seek help and engage in this workbook is itself an act of protection for your children. Every step you take toward your own healing and stabilization is a step toward creating a safer, healthier environment for them.

Before You Move On:

Module 10 addresses perhaps the hardest question in this workbook: what to do — stay or leave. This module does not tell you what to decide. It gives you a framework for making the most informed, values-aligned decision possible. Continue when you are ready.

Module 10

Making Difficult Decisions — Staying or Leaving

Clinical Rationale: Among the most agonizing decisions a family member of a gambler faces is whether to stay in or leave the relationship. This is not a decision that any workbook — or any clinician — should make for you. What this module provides is a structured, evidence-based framework for examining this decision with clarity, courage, and honest self-knowledge. Whatever you decide, you deserve to make that decision with your eyes fully open.

What You Will Gain from This Module

- A non-judgmental framework for examining the staying/leaving decision
- An MI-based decisional balance worksheet for both partners and parents
- Safety planning guidance and warning signs for intimate partner violence
- Practical guidance for both "staying with conditions" and "leaving safely"
- A values clarification exercise to ground your decision in your deepest commitments

10.1 The Hardest Question: Should I Stay or Should I Go?

There is no universally right answer to this question. Factors including physical safety, children's welfare, financial entanglement, length of relationship, the gambler's level of commitment to change, cultural and religious values, and your own inner sense of what you can sustain — all interact in ways that no formula can resolve.

What this module affirms is this: **you have the right to make this decision, whatever it is.** Staying is not weakness. Leaving is not abandonment. Making no decision right now is also valid. The goal is simply to make your eventual decision — whenever it comes — from the most grounded, informed, and self-aware position possible.

> **A Note on Non-Judgment**
>
> This module does not advocate for leaving or staying. Both decisions involve real costs and real benefits. Both decisions can be made from a place of love, clarity, and values alignment. Both decisions require ongoing support. You are the only one who knows the full complexity of your situation.

10.2 Decision-Making Framework — The Balance Sheet

WORKSHEET 10.2 — Decisional Balance Worksheet (For Spouses / Partners)

Instructions: Complete all four quadrants honestly. Take your time. This is not about counting columns — it is about gaining clarity on what is at stake and what you truly value.

Reasons to STAY (Benefits of Staying)	**Reasons to LEAVE (Benefits of Leaving)**
What do I gain or preserve by staying?	What do I gain or protect by leaving?
Costs of Staying	**Costs of Leaving**
What do I give up or risk if I stay?	What do I give up or risk if I leave?

Looking at this balance sheet, what strikes you most?

What value or concern carries the most weight for you personally?

WORKSHEET 10.2B — Decisional Balance (For Parents of Adult Gamblers)

Benefits of Maintaining Relationship as Is	Benefits of Significantly Limiting Contact / Support
Costs of Maintaining Relationship as Is	**Costs of Limiting Contact / Support**

10.3 Safety Planning — When Staying Is Dangerous

Safety Alert — Please Read Carefully

Research documents a significant overlap between problem gambling and intimate partner violence (IPV). Financial desperation, shame, and emotional dysregulation associated with gambling disorder can increase the risk of controlling, threatening, or physically violent behavior. If any of the warning signs below apply to your situation, please contact the National Domestic Violence Hotline at **1-800-799-7233** before making any major decision.

Warning Signs of Dangerous Situations in Gambling Households

- Physical threats, intimidation, or violence — past or present
- Extreme controlling behavior around finances, movement, or communication
- Threats of harm to you, the children, or the gambler themselves if you try to leave
- Isolation from family and friends
- Escalating emotional volatility or rage episodes
- Threats related to custody of children

Basic Safety Planning Steps

16. Identify a safe person you can go to at any time without explanation
17. Keep important documents (ID, passport, birth certificates, financial records) in a secure, accessible location
18. Have a go-bag prepared if physical safety is a concern
19. Know the location of the nearest domestic violence shelter
20. Have the National DV Hotline number saved: **1-800-799-7233**
21. Consult with a legal aid attorney about your rights

10.4 If You Choose to Stay — Creating a Sustainable Plan

Choosing to stay in a relationship with an active gambler — or choosing to remain in relationship with a gambling-addicted family member — does not have to mean accepting the status quo. Staying with conditions and with intention is a very different thing from staying passively.

Conditions for a Sustainable Staying Plan

- Engagement in your own individual therapy or Gam-Anon support
- Clear, written agreements about financial transparency

- Specific milestones or timelines for the gambler to engage with treatment
- Pre-determined consequences that you are prepared to follow through on
- Access to couples or family therapy
- A private support network for yourself
- Regular re-evaluation of whether the plan is sustainable

10.5 If You Choose to Leave — The Exit Plan

WORKSHEET 10.5 — Exit Planning Checklist

For partners and spouses considering or planning separation. Complete at your own pace.

☐	Step	Completed / Target Date
☐	Consult a family law attorney (many offer free initial consultations)	________
☐	Separate all financial accounts and direct deposit	________
☐	Secure copies of important documents (mortgage, birth certificates, tax returns, loan agreements)	________
☐	Identify and secure housing options	________
☐	Arrange children's schooling and care transitions	________
☐	Build your personal financial safety net (individual account, budget)	________
☐	Identify your personal support system for the transition	________
☐	Begin or continue individual therapy to support the transition	________
☐	Allow yourself to grieve the relationship while also moving forward	________

10.6 Reflection Exercise: My Values Compass

Reflection Exercise 10.6 — Values Clarification

Instructions: Review the values listed below. In Step 1, circle your top 10. In Step 2, narrow to your top 5. In Step 3, identify your top 3 core values. Then reflect on the questions below.

Values List: Honesty · Loyalty · Safety · Freedom · Love · Family · Children's Well-being · Financial Security · Integrity · Peace · Adventure · Stability · Independence · Faith/Spirituality · Connection · Authenticity · Courage · Compassion · Self-Respect · Justice · Health · Joy · Growth · Community · Trust · Forgiveness · Partnership · Personal Achievement · Privacy · Service to Others · Hope · Patience · Kindness · Respect · Fun · Creativity · Wisdom · Humor · Presence · Balance

My Top 10 Values:

My Top 5 Values:

My Top 3 Core Values:

How well does your current situation — and your current decisions — reflect these core values?

What decision — regarding staying or leaving — would most honor your core values?

Module 10 Summary

The decision to stay or leave a relationship affected by gambling addiction is deeply personal, profoundly complex, and entirely yours to make. What this module has offered is a framework for making that decision from a place of clarity, honest self-assessment, and values alignment — rather than from panic, exhaustion, or an incomplete picture of the options. Whatever you decide, you deserve support.

Before You Move On:

Module 11 is entirely devoted to you — your self-care, your support network, and the recovery of the life and identity that existed before gambling took over. This may be the most important module in the workbook. Continue when you are ready.

Module 11

Self-Care, Support, and Building Your Own Life

Clinical Rationale: Self-care is not a luxury in the context of chronic caregiver stress and secondary trauma — it is a clinical necessity. Research on caregiver burnout, secondary traumatic stress, and compassion fatigue consistently demonstrates that family members who neglect their own well-being become less effective in every domain of their lives, including in their ability to support others. This module is a declaration that your life, your health, and your well-being matter — not as an afterthought, but as the foundation of everything else.

What You Will Gain from This Module

- A reframe of self-care as a clinical necessity, not selfishness
- A comprehensive self-care inventory across six life domains
- Practical information about Gam-Anon and other peer support resources
- A visual support network mapping exercise
- A weekly self-care planning tool
- A guided identity reclamation exercise

11.1 You Cannot Pour from an Empty Cup — The Case for Self-Care

The oxygen mask analogy is used in clinical training for good reason: on an airplane, you are instructed to secure your own oxygen mask before assisting others — because an unconscious caregiver cannot help anyone. The same principle applies to family members of people with addiction. When you are depleted, traumatized, financially ruined, and emotionally empty, your capacity to make good decisions, hold boundaries, communicate effectively, and care for children is severely compromised.

Self-care in this context is not bubble baths and scented candles (though those are fine too). It is the full-spectrum maintenance of the physical, emotional, social, spiritual, creative, and professional dimensions of your own life — the parts of yourself that existed before gambling became the center of your world, and that can exist again.

Research on caregiver burnout demonstrates that individuals who maintain even modest levels of self-care — one regular social connection, one physical health practice, one meaningful activity — show significantly better outcomes in both their own mental health and their capacity to navigate their caregiving role effectively.

11.2 The Self-Care Inventory

WORKSHEET 11.2 — My Self-Care Inventory

Instructions: For each item, rate your current engagement using 1 = Not at all through 5 = Regularly and consistently. Then identify gaps — areas where you would like to do more.

Domain 1: Physical Self-Care

Practice	1	2	3	4	5
Getting 7–8 hours of sleep most nights	1	2	3	4	5
Eating regular, nutritious meals	1	2	3	4	5
Engaging in physical exercise or movement	1	2	3	4	5
Attending routine medical and dental appointments	1	2	3	4	5

Practice	1	2	3	4	5
Limiting alcohol, caffeine, and substances	1	2	3	4	5

Domain 2: Emotional Self-Care

Practice	1	2	3	4	5
Processing emotions through journaling, therapy, or trusted conversation	1	2	3	4	5
Setting and maintaining emotional boundaries	1	2	3	4	5
Allowing yourself to feel difficult emotions without suppression	1	2	3	4	5
Practicing self-compassion when you make mistakes	1	2	3	4	5
Engaging in practices that bring you comfort (music, nature, art)	1	2	3	4	5

Domain 3: Social Self-Care

Practice	1	2	3	4	5
Maintaining at least one close friendship	1	2	3	4	5
Participating in support groups (Gam-Anon, Al-Anon)	1	2	3	4	5
Engaging in community or faith-based connection	1	2	3	4	5
Setting aside time for socializing separate from family crisis	1	2	3	4	5

Domain 4: Spiritual / Meaning Self-Care

Practice	1	2	3	4	5
Engaging in prayer, meditation, or mindfulness practice	1	2	3	4	5

Practice	1	2	3	4	5
Finding meaning or purpose outside the gambling situation	1	2	3	4	5
Connecting with nature or a sense of something larger	1	2	3	4	5
Practicing gratitude, however small	1	2	3	4	5

Domain 5: Professional / Creative Self-Care

Practice	1	2	3	4	5
Maintaining professional engagement or pursuing career goals	1	2	3	4	5
Engaging in creative activities (art, music, writing, cooking)	1	2	3	4	5
Learning new skills or pursuing personal development	1	2	3	4	5

Domain 6: Recreational Self-Care

Practice	1	2	3	4	5
Engaging in hobbies or leisure activities regularly	1	2	3	4	5
Taking time off or vacationing (even in small doses)	1	2	3	4	5
Laughing — finding moments of genuine humor and lightness	1	2	3	4	5

Domain where I am strongest: ____

Domain I most need to develop: ____

One specific self-care practice I will start this week: _________________________________

____

11.3 Gam-Anon and Other Support Resources

Gam-Anon is a peer support fellowship for family members, friends, and loved ones of people with gambling problems. Based on a 12-Step model adapted from Al-Anon, Gam-Anon meetings provide a confidential, non-judgmental space where family members can share their experiences, gain perspective, and receive support from others who truly understand.

What to Expect at a First Gam-Anon Meeting

- Meetings are free and open to anyone affected by a loved one's gambling
- You are never required to share — you can simply listen
- Meetings are confidential — what is shared in the room stays in the room
- You may hear stories that resonate powerfully with your own experience
- Some meetings are available online (visit gam-anon.org for listings)

Additional Support Options

Resource	Best For	Contact
Gam-Anon	Ongoing peer support for family members of gamblers; 12-Step based	www.gam-anon.org
Al-Anon	When gambling is concurrent with alcohol or other substance use	www.al-anon.org
Individual Therapy	Personalized clinical support; trauma processing; CBT and MI	Psychology Today directory; therapist referral from primary care
SMART Recovery Family & Friends	Science-based, non-12-Step alternative for family members	www.smartrecovery.org
Online Support Communities	Anonymous peer connection for those in rural areas or without local resources	Reddit r/problemgambling; Gambling Therapy (gamblingtherapy.org)

11.4 Worksheet: Building My Support Network Map

WORKSHEET 11.4 — My Support Network Map

Instructions: In the concentric circles below, place names of people and resources that support you. Inner circle = closest, most trusted; Middle = helpful connections; Outer = community resources and broader supports.

	MIDDLE CIRCLE *(Helpful connections — I can reach out when needed)*	OUTER CIRCLE *(Community resources — professionals, groups, programs)*
Names:	Names:	Resources:

What gaps do you notice in your support network?

One step I will take this week to strengthen my support network:

11.5 My Weekly Self-Care Plan

MY WEEKLY SELF-CARE PLAN

Day	Self-Care Commitment	Domain	Did I do it? ☐
Monday			☐

Day	Self-Care Commitment	Domain	Did I do it? ☐
Tuesday			☐
Wednesday			☐
Thursday			☐
Friday			☐
Saturday			☐
Sunday			☐

End of week reflection: What worked? What was hard? What will I adjust next week?

11.6 Reflection Exercise: Who Was I Before All This?

Reflection Exercise 11.6 — Identity Reclamation

"Before the gambling took over, I used to..."

"Things I loved that I have given up or set aside..."

"One thing I want to reclaim is..."

"The person I am becoming — the one I am choosing, on purpose — is..."

Module 11 Summary

You are a whole person — not simply a family member of a gambler. Your needs, your health, your relationships, your passions, and your identity deserve attention and investment. Self-care in the context of this experience is not self-indulgence; it is the act of preserving the person that everyone around you needs — especially you.

Before You Move On:

Module 12 addresses the possibility of your loved one seeking help — and what your role looks like in that process. This module is filled with hope, realistic expectation, and practical guidance. Continue when you are ready.

Module 12

Supporting Recovery — If Your Loved One Seeks Help

Clinical Rationale: The process of supporting a loved one who enters recovery is as nuanced and demanding as any other aspect of the gambling experience — perhaps more so. Family members often arrive at this stage with deep hope, alongside equally deep exhaustion and wariness born of previous disappointment. This module provides a realistic, evidence-based, and compassionate framework for the recovery support role — one that protects your own well-being while genuinely supporting your loved one's process.

What You Will Gain from This Module

- Realistic expectations for what the early recovery process looks like
- CRAFT-based guidance on your role as a recovery supporter
- A framework for understanding trust repair as a process over time
- A collaborative Recovery Support Agreement worksheet
- Guidance on couples and family therapy
- A future-oriented visualization and writing exercise grounded in hope

12.1 Understanding the Recovery Process

Recovery from gambling disorder is real, achievable, and well-documented in clinical research. But it is rarely linear, and family members who go into the process with unrealistic expectations are at high risk for devastating disappointment when the normal difficulties of recovery occur.

The Stages of Change Model (Prochaska & DiClemente)

Stage	What It Looks Like	Your Role
Precontemplation	The gambler does not yet see gambling as a problem	Reduce enabling; allow natural consequences; maintain boundaries
Contemplation	Ambivalent — sees some problems but not ready for change	Reflect their stated concerns without lecturing; provide information
Preparation	Beginning to consider or plan for change	Reinforce motivation; offer support without taking over
Action	Actively engaged in treatment or behavioral change	Warm, consistent support; observe changed behavior (not just words)
Maintenance	Sustaining change over time; managing triggers and relapse risk	Support ongoing engagement; maintain your own self-care and boundaries
Relapse	Return to gambling — a common and expected part of the recovery process	Do not catastrophize; return to boundaries; encourage re-engagement with treatment

Relapse Is Not Failure

Clinical research consistently identifies relapse as a common event in the recovery process — not a sign that recovery is impossible. The average person with a substance or behavioral addiction makes multiple attempts before achieving sustained recovery. Relapse does not erase progress; it provides important information about triggers and vulnerabilities. Your role is not to prevent relapse but to maintain your own boundaries and encourage the gambler to return to their recovery plan.

12.2 Your Role in Their Recovery — Helpful and Harmful

The CRAFT model provides specific guidance on how family members can support the recovery process without sliding back into enabling. The central distinction is this: **reward recovery behaviors warmly and consistently; disengage from gambling behaviors without reinforcing them.**

Helpful Recovery Support	Harmful / Enabling Behaviors to Avoid
Acknowledging and celebrating sober days and recovery milestones genuinely	Rewarding promises rather than demonstrated behavioral changes
Offering to attend a counseling session together	Making excuses to the gambler's counselor or treatment provider
Maintaining your own therapy and support group attendance	Dropping your own support "now that they're getting help"
Engaging in positive, shared activities when the gambler is not gambling	Resuming full financial trust before it has been rebuilt through consistent behavior
Expressing genuine care and connection in the relationship	Weaponizing past gambling against them during arguments about unrelated topics
Maintaining established boundaries even in recovery	Pretending everything is fine before trust has genuinely been rebuilt
Developing a written relapse plan together	Panicking or catastrophizing if a slip occurs

12.3 Rebuilding Trust — A Realistic Timeline

One of the most common sources of conflict in the early recovery phase is the mismatch between the gambler's timeline for trust restoration and the family member's. The gambler, often experiencing newfound clarity and motivation, may feel that because they have stopped gambling, trust should return quickly. The family member, carrying years of broken promises and financial trauma, needs to see consistent behavior over time before trust can genuinely rebuild.

Both experiences are valid. Both deserve to be spoken.

The Trust Rebuilding Framework

- **Trust is earned through consistent behavior over time** — not through promises, apologies, or good intentions
- **Financial transparency is non-negotiable** in early recovery — access to statements, shared financial planning, and accountability structures
- **Forgiveness and trust are separate processes** — you can choose to forgive without yet extending trust; forgiveness is for your own healing, trust is earned through behavior
- **Set specific, behavioral trust benchmarks** — not vague feelings but measurable actions: "After 90 days of consistent treatment attendance and financial transparency, I will reconsider joint account access."
- **Trust repair takes months to years** for significant betrayals — normalizing this timeline for both parties reduces resentment and unrealistic expectations

12.4 Worksheet: My Recovery Support Agreement

WORKSHEET 12.4 — Recovery Support Agreement

This worksheet is designed to be completed collaboratively with the gambler in a conjoint therapy session or in a structured, calm conversation. Both parties should agree to all items and sign below.

Date: ______________________ **Location / Therapist present:** ______________________

Shared Goals for Recovery

What we both want for our relationship and family:

The Gambler's Commitments

Commitment	Specific Behavioral Terms	Timeline
Treatment / Counseling attendance		
Financial transparency		
GA / treatment program participation		
Communication commitments		
Other: ____________________		

The Family Member's Commitments

Commitment	Specific Behavioral Terms
Ongoing self-care and support group participation	
Agreed-upon positive reinforcement of recovery behaviors	
Agreed-upon response if relapse occurs	
Other: ____________________	

Relapse Plan — If Gambling Occurs Again

If relapse occurs, we agree to:

Weekly Check-In

We agree to a weekly check-in on: **Day:** ____________ **Time:** ____________ **Format:** ____________

Gambler's Signature: **Date:** ____________

Family Member's Signature: **Date:** ____________

Therapist / Witness: **Date:** ____________

12.5 Couples and Family Therapy — When and How

Professional couples and family therapy is a powerful complement to individual treatment for gambling disorder — but timing matters. Couples therapy during active, unaddressed gambling is generally not recommended, as the deception and power imbalances that characterize active addiction make productive therapeutic work very difficult. Once the gambler has engaged with individual treatment and achieved some initial stability, couples therapy becomes a valuable arena for trust repair, communication rebuilding, and relational healing.

What to Look for in a Therapist

- Experience with addiction and its impact on families
- Training in evidence-based couples modalities (Gottman Method, Emotionally Focused Therapy, or CRAFT)
- Knowledge of gambling disorder specifically (look for ICGC or similar credentials)
- A non-judgmental, trauma-informed approach
- Willingness to see individual partners separately as well as together

> **Red Flags in Couples Therapy Contexts**
>
> Avoid therapists who: pressure you to stay in the relationship; dismiss your trauma responses as "overreaction"; treat the family member's boundaries as the problem; or conduct couples therapy while the gambling disorder remains completely unaddressed.

12.6 Reflection Exercise: My Vision for Our Future

Reflection Exercise 12.6 — A Future Worth Imagining

Research in Motivational Interviewing identifies future-oriented hope as one of the most powerful drivers of behavioral change — for the gambler and for you. The following exercise invites you to envision a future in which recovery has taken hold. Even if it feels distant or uncertain, allow yourself to imagine it.

One year from now, if recovery is holding:

What does your home feel like?

What does your relationship look like?

Three years from now:

Where are you financially?

How are the children (if applicable)?

Five years from now:

What does your life look like — your own life, apart from the recovery story?

What is one step you can take today toward that five-year vision?

Module 12 Summary

If your loved one chooses recovery, your journey is not over — it is entering a new and nuanced phase. Supporting recovery well requires that you continue caring for yourself, maintaining clear expectations, celebrating genuine progress, and holding realistic timelines for trust repair. Hope is not naive; in the context of recovery, it is clinically powerful. And whatever the outcome for your loved one, your own recovery, your own healing, and your own future deserve every ounce of the energy and care you have poured into others.

A Final Word

You have done something remarkable by completing this workbook. You have faced your experience honestly, examined painful patterns with courage, and invested in your own healing. Whatever lies ahead — recovery, continued struggle, decisions not yet made — you are better equipped than when you began. Keep going. You deserve a life that is fully your own.

— James Martinez, MS, LCADC, LSATP, CAADC, CASAC-II, ICGC

Appendices

Appendix A: National and Local Resources

National Council on Problem Gambling (NCPG) Helpline
24/7 confidential helpline for problem gamblers and their families.
Phone: 1-800-522-4700 | **Text:** "GAMBLER" to 833234 | **Chat:** www.ncpgambling.org

Gam-Anon International Service Office
Peer support fellowship for families and loved ones of problem gamblers.
Website: www.gam-anon.org | Find local and online meetings through the website

Gamblers Anonymous International Service Office
12-Step fellowship for individuals with gambling problems.
Website: www.gamblersanonymous.org | **Phone:** 1-800-367-8461

National Domestic Violence Hotline
24/7 confidential support for those experiencing domestic violence.

Phone: 1-800-799-7233 (SAFE) | **TTY:** 1-800-787-3224 | **Text:** "START" to 88788 | **Chat:** www.thehotline.org

SAMHSA National Helpline
Substance Abuse and Mental Health Services Administration — free, confidential treatment referral service.
Phone: 1-800-662-4357 (HELP) | **TTY:** 1-800-487-4889 | **Website:** www.samhsa.gov/find-help/national-helpline

National Foundation for Credit Counseling (NFCC)
Non-profit financial counseling and debt management services nationwide.
Phone: 1-800-388-2227 | **Website:** www.nfcc.org

SMART Recovery Family & Friends
Science-based, non-12-Step support for family members and loved ones of individuals with addiction.
Website: www.smartrecovery.org/family

Gambling Therapy (International)
Free online support for problem gamblers and their families — includes forums, live chat, and self-help tools.
Website: www.gamblingtherapy.org

Al-Anon Family Groups

Peer support for families and friends of alcoholics — also relevant when gambling co-occurs with alcohol use.

Phone: 1-888-425-2666 | **Website:** www.al-anon.org

National Legal Aid & Defender Association

Find local legal aid offices for individuals needing free or low-cost legal counsel related to debt, bankruptcy, or family law.

Website: www.nlada.org

Crisis Text Line

Free, 24/7 crisis support via text message for anyone in emotional distress.

Text: HOME to 741741

988 Suicide & Crisis Lifeline

If you or someone you love is in immediate crisis or expressing suicidal thoughts.

Call or Text: 988 | **Chat:** www.988lifeline.org

Note for Clinicians

State-level problem gambling councils and councils on compulsive gambling maintain regional referral lists that may include gambling-specific therapists, treatment programs, and family support groups not listed here. Encourage clients to contact their state council for local resources.

Appendix B: Glossary of Clinical Terms

The following terms are used throughout this workbook. Definitions are written in plain language for accessibility.

Adverse Childhood Experiences (ACE)

Stressful or traumatic events occurring in childhood — including household dysfunction, abuse, neglect, and parental addiction — that have been linked to lifelong impacts on physical health, mental health, and life outcomes. Research demonstrates that children of problem gamblers are at elevated ACE risk.

Boundaries

Clear, specific statements of what a person will and will not accept in a relationship, along with pre-determined consequences if those limits are violated. In clinical work, boundaries are understood as acts of self-respect that protect well-being and create the conditions for healthy relating.

Cognitive Behavioral Therapy (CBT)

An evidence-based therapeutic approach that focuses on identifying and modifying the relationships between thoughts, emotions, and behaviors. In the context of gambling family work, CBT is used to target automatic thoughts that drive enabling, self-blame, shame, and avoidance.

Codependency

A pattern of excessive emotional and behavioral focus on another person's needs, problems, or addiction — typically at significant cost to one's own well-being, autonomy, and sense of self. Codependency in addiction families develops as an adaptive response to chronic relational instability.

Community Reinforcement and Family Training (CRAFT)

An evidence-based behavioral approach designed to help concerned significant others (CSOs) — family members and close friends of individuals with addiction — reduce enabling, improve their own quality of life, and use positive reinforcement and strategic communication to motivate their loved one to enter treatment. CRAFT has strong empirical support across substance use and behavioral addictions.

Compassion Fatigue

A state of emotional, physical, and psychological exhaustion that results from prolonged caregiving or exposure to others' suffering. Related to Secondary Traumatic Stress, compassion fatigue is common in family members of individuals with active addiction.

Decisional Balance

A Motivational Interviewing tool that helps individuals explore the costs and benefits of a particular behavior or decision — in both directions. Used in Module 10 to help family members examine the staying-or-leaving decision with honesty and clarity.

Disenfranchised Grief

Grief that is not acknowledged, validated, or supported by social norms because it does not fit the traditional model of bereavement. Family members of gamblers frequently experience disenfranchised grief — mourning the relationship they thought they had, the person their loved one used to be, and the future they expected — without social permission to grieve openly.

Enabling

Any behavior by a family member that shields the person with addiction from experiencing the natural consequences of their behavior — and in doing so, inadvertently reduces motivation for change. Enabling is almost always motivated by love and fear, not by indifference to consequences.

Family Systems Theory

A clinical framework that understands the family as an interdependent system in which each member's behavior affects and is affected by every other member. In addiction work, family systems theory explains how gambling disorder produces role adaptations, communication distortions, and systemic dysfunction throughout the entire family unit.

Hypervigilance

A state of chronic, heightened alertness in which the nervous system is continuously scanning for threat or danger. In gambling-affected families, hypervigilance develops as an adaptive response to unpredictability and repeated crisis. It is a recognized symptom of trauma and PTSD.

Locus of Control

A psychological construct referring to a person's belief about whether outcomes in their life are primarily determined by their own actions (internal locus) or by external forces such as other people, chance, or circumstances (external locus). Family members of gamblers often experience a shift toward an external locus of control, feeling that their lives are governed by the gambler's behavior.

Cognitive Distortion

An inaccurate or irrational pattern of thinking that influences emotions and behavior. Gamblers experience specific cognitive distortions around gambling (e.g., the gambler's fallacy, magical thinking about winning). Family members often develop their own cognitive distortions, including catastrophizing, all-or-nothing thinking, and excessive self-blame.

Motivational Interviewing (MI)

A collaborative, person-centered counseling approach designed to strengthen an individual's own motivation for and commitment to change. MI uses open-ended questions, reflective listening, affirmations, and summaries to explore ambivalence and elicit change talk. The Decisional Balance and future visualization exercises in this workbook are MI-derived.

Parentification

A role reversal in which a child is expected to fulfill adult responsibilities — emotional or instrumental — within the family system. In gambling-affected households, children may be parentified by taking on household management tasks, monitoring the gambler, or serving as emotional support for the non-gambling parent.

Protective Factor

A strength, resource, or condition that reduces the risk of negative outcomes and supports resilience in individuals and families. Examples in the gambling context include social support, access to mental health services, financial literacy, and strong parenting by the non-gambling caregiver.

Recovery Capital

The total set of internal and external resources that an individual can draw upon to support their recovery from addiction. Includes personal strengths, social support, housing stability, financial resources, health, and community connection. Clinicians use this concept to assess recovery readiness and support planning.

Relapse

A return to problematic gambling behavior after a period of abstinence or reduced gambling. Relapse is understood in contemporary addiction medicine as a common event in the recovery process — not a sign of failure or proof that recovery is impossible. Effective relapse planning is a standard component of gambling disorder treatment.

Secondary Traumatic Stress (STS)

Trauma symptoms that develop in a person as a result of close, prolonged exposure to another person's trauma, crisis, or suffering. Also referred to as vicarious trauma or compassion fatigue, STS is well-documented in family members of individuals with addiction and in professional caregivers.

Solution-Focused Therapy

A brief, strengths-based therapeutic approach that focuses on identifying what is working and building toward a desired future — rather than dwelling extensively on problems, history, or pathology. Solution-Focused principles inform the future visualization exercises and strengths-based framing throughout this workbook.

Trauma-Informed Care (TIC)

A clinical framework that recognizes the widespread impact of trauma, integrates knowledge about trauma into clinical practice, and prioritizes physical and psychological safety, trustworthiness, choice, collaboration, and empowerment in service delivery. TIC informs the overall tone, structure, and safety orientation of this workbook.

Appendix C: Suggested Reading and References

The following references represent key empirical and clinical works that informed the development of this workbook. They are provided in APA format for clinicians and interested readers seeking deeper engagement with the evidence base.

American Psychiatric Association. (2013). *Diagnostic and statistical manual of mental disorders* (5th ed.). American Psychiatric Publishing.

Boughton, R., & Falenchuk, O. (2007). Vulnerability and comorbidity factors in female problem gambling. *Journal of Gambling Studies, 23*(3), 323–334. https://doi.org/10.1007/s10899-007-9056-6

Blaszczynski, A., & Nower, L. (2002). A pathways model of problem and pathological gambling. *Addiction, 97*(5), 487–499. https://doi.org/10.1046/j.1360-0443.2002.00015.x

Copello, A., Velleman, R., & Templeton, L. (2005). Family interventions in the treatment of alcohol and drug problems. *Drug and Alcohol Review, 24*(4), 369–385. https://doi.org/10.1080/09595230500302356

Delfabbro, P., & King, D. L. (2012). Relative harms associated with gaming and gambling: An analysis of the evidence and implications for harm minimisation. *Australian & New Zealand Journal of Public Health, 36*(2), 124–129.

Felitti, V. J., Anda, R. F., Nordenberg, D., Williamson, D. F., Spitz, A. M., Edwards, V., Koss, M. P., & Marks, J. S. (1998). Relationship of childhood abuse and household dysfunction to many of the leading causes of death in adults. *American Journal of Preventive Medicine, 14*(4), 245–258.

Fontes, M. A., Breen, R. B., Bhavsar, V., & Bhugra, D. (2021). Problem gambling and intimate partner violence: A systematic review. *Journal of Gambling Studies, 37*(1), 1–22. https://doi.org/10.1007/s10899-020-09952-1

Herman, J. L. (1992). *Trauma and recovery: The aftermath of violence — from domestic abuse to political terror.* Basic Books.

Hodgins, D. C., Shead, N. W., & Makarchuk, K. (2007). Relationship satisfaction and psychological distress among concerned significant others of pathological gamblers. *Journal of Nervous and Mental Disease, 195*(1), 65–71.

Landau, J., Stanton, M. D., Brinkman-Sull, D., Ikle, D., McCormick, D., Garrett, J., Baciewicz, G., Shea, R. R., Browning, A., & Wamboldt, F. (2004). Outcomes with the ARISE approach to engaging reluctant drug and alcohol-dependent individuals in treatment. *The American Journal of Drug and Alcohol Abuse, 30*(4), 711–748.

Lesieur, H. R., & Blume, S. B. (1987). The South Oaks Gambling Screen (SOGS): A new instrument for the identification of pathological gamblers. *American Journal of Psychiatry, 144*(9), 1184–1188.

Lorenz, V. C., & Shuttlesworth, D. E. (1983). The impact of pathological gambling on the spouse of the gambler. *Journal of Community Psychology, 11*(1), 67–76.

Meyers, R. J., & Wolfe, B. L. (2004). *Get your loved one sober: Alternatives to nagging, pleading, and threatening.* Hazelden Publishing.

Miller, W. R., & Rollnick, S. (2013). *Motivational interviewing: Helping people change* (3rd ed.). Guilford Press.

Petry, N. M. (2005). *Pathological gambling: Etiology, comorbidity, and treatment.* American Psychological Association.

Prochaska, J. O., DiClemente, C. C., & Norcross, J. C. (1992). In search of how people change: Applications to addictive behaviors. *American Psychologist, 47*(9), 1102–1114.

Rychtarik, R. G., & McGillicuddy, N. B. (2006). Coping skills training and 12-step facilitation for women whose partner has alcoholism: Effects on depression, the partner's drinking, and partner physical violence. *Journal of Consulting and Clinical Psychology, 74*(4), 628–638.

Shaffer, H. J., & Korn, D. A. (2002). Gambling and related mental disorders: A public health analysis. *Annual Review of Public Health, 23*, 171–212.

Shead, N. W., Derevensky, J. L., & Gupta, R. (2010). Risk and protective factors associated with youth problem gambling. *International Journal of Adolescent Medicine and Health, 22*(1), 39–58.

Smith, J. E., & Meyers, R. J. (2004). *Motivating substance abusers to enter treatment: Working with family members.* Guilford Press.

Steinberg, M. A., Kosten, T. A., & Rounsaville, B. J. (1992). Cocaine abuse and pathological gambling. *The American Journal on Addictions, 1*(2), 121–132.

Velleman, R., Templeton, L. J., & Copello, A. G. (2005). The role of the family in preventing and intervening with substance use and misuse: A comprehensive review of family interventions. *Drug and Alcohol Review, 24*(2), 93–109.

Whiting, S. W., Dixon, M. R., & Wilson, A. N. (2018). The family member of the problem gambler: A review of the evidence and theory of behavior change. *Journal of Gambling Studies, 34*(3), 847–866.

Note: Clinicians seeking additional peer-reviewed resources on gambling disorder and family treatment are encouraged to consult the ***Journal of Gambling Studies****, the National Council on Problem Gambling research library, and the Society for Research on Gambling academic resources.*

Appendix D: Notes Pages

Use the following pages for additional journaling, notes, or personal reflections as you work through the modules.

Notes —

Notes —

LIVING IN THE SHADOW OF THE BET

A Clinical Workbook for Families Affected by Gambling Addiction

James Martinez, MS, LCADC, LSATP, CAADC, CASAC-II, ICGC

Stress Free Recovery LLC

Series: Evidence-Based Clinical Frameworks

Workbook Edition · 8.5 × 11 in · United States

www.ingramcontent.com/pod-product-compliance
Lightning Source LLC
LaVergne TN
LVHW060452061126
851857LV00016B/1802